*"I came so that they might have life
and have it more abundantly."*

John 10:10

Contents

Bridges to Faith

Essentials of the Catholic Faith for Children Ages 8–11

JOE PAPROCKI, D.Min.

LOYOLAPRESS.
A JESUIT MINISTRY

IMPRIMATUR

In accordance with c. 827, permission to publish is granted on May 23, 2012 by Rev. Msgr. John F. Canary, Vicar General of the Archdiocese of Chicago. Permission to publish is an official declaration of ecclesiastical authority that the material is free from doctrinal and moral error. No legal responsibility is assumed by the grant of this permission.

Bridges to Faith is an expression of the work of Loyola Press, a ministry of the Society of Jesus, the Jesuits.

Author: Joe Paprocki, D.Min.
Cover design: Loyola Press
Cover Illustration: Penelope Dullaghan
Interior design: Loyola Press

ISBN-13: 978-0-8294-3747-8
ISBN-10: 0-8294-3747-9

Copyright © 2014 Loyola Press, Chicago, IL.

LOYOLAPRESS.
A JESUIT MINISTRY

3441 N. Ashland Avenue
Chicago, Illinois 60657
(800) 621-1008

www.loyolapress.com
www.bridges-to-faith.com

Printed in the United States of America
19 20 21 22 23 LSC 10 9 8 7 6 5 4 3

Art Acknowledgements

1 ©Pavel Bolotov/Getty Images/ Thinkstock. **6** ©Penelope Dullaghan. **9** ©iStockphoto.com/rhoon. **11** ©BejhanJusufi/ Thinkstock. **15** ©iStockphoto/ Thinkstock. **21**(b) ©iStockphoto.com/ LokFung. **21**(t) ©iStockphoto.com/ dra_schwartz. **27** ©iStockphoto.com/ jammydesign. **33** ©iStockphoto.com/ jammydesign. **39** ©iStockphoto.com/ albertc111. **49** ©iStockphoto.com/Leontura. **53** ©Vitali Konstantinov. **54** ©Yoshi Miyake. **57** ©iStockphoto.com/jammydesign. **63** ©Bocman1973/Shutterstock.com. **71** ©Philomena O'Neill. **71**(c) ©Philomena O'Neill. **71**(r) ©Philomena O'Neill. **73** ©iStockphoto. com/A-Digit. **79** ©iStockphoto.com/MarinaMM. **81** ©iStockphoto.com/jammydesign. **85** ©iStockphoto/Thinkstock. **91** ©iStockphoto.com/ A-Digit. **97** ©iStockphoto.com/LokFung. **101** ©iStockphoto.com/Link-creative. **107** ©iStockphoto.com/bubaone. **111**(l) ©iStockphoto.com/KathrynKirsch. **111**(r) ©iStockphoto/Thinkstock. **113** ©iStockphoto.com/bpowelldesign. **115** ©iStockphoto.com/A-Digit. **123** ©iStockphoto/ Thinkstock. **131** ©iStockphoto.com/osadzena. **135** ©Greg Kuepfer. **136**(a) ©Yoshi Miyake. **136**(b) ©Yoshi Miyake. **136**(c) ©Yoshi Miyake. **136**(d) ©Yoshi Miyake. **141** ©iStockphoto.com/ bubaone

Part 4—Prayer: Praying Faith

Introduction

When families go on a driving vacation, one of the fun things that can happen is driving on a long bridge over a river. It's fun to look down to see the water below, to look back to see the land you left behind, and to look ahead to see the land you are about to enter. Bridges connect the past—where we've been—to the future—where we are heading. This book, *Bridges to Faith*, is going to do the same thing for you. It's going to connect you with your past and with a future that brings you closer to Jesus Christ.

Without a bridge, we can get stuck in one place. Without a bridge, we can find ourselves in danger from the rough waters beneath us. As you grow older, it is important to have bridges in your life—ways to help you move forward and not get stuck in one place, as well as safeguards from the rough waters that you may face. The Catholic faith can be that bridge for you. The teachings and practices of the Catholic Church will help you move forward in life, growing closer to Jesus while keeping you safe from the dangers of sin.

Crossing a bridge can sometimes be a little scary. Don't be afraid. The bridge you are about to cross is made of very strong materials: the Creed (what we believe), the sacraments (how we worship), moral life (how we show love to one another) and prayer (how we talk and listen to God). This bridge is held up by the love of God and held together by the faith of many people—parents, family members, godparents, teachers, priests, nuns, and saints—whose faith acts like steel bolts welded together to reinforce the bridge's strength.

Jesus is calling to you to cross the bridge of faith and to come closer to him so that you may walk together every day of your life and for all eternity.

Joe Paprocki

Joe Paprocki, D.Min.

National Consultant for Faith Formation, Loyola Press

PART 1

The Creed: Holding On to Faith

Then Jesus approached and said to them, "All power in heaven and on earth has been given to me. Go, therefore, and make disciples of all nations, baptizing them in the name of the Father, and of the Son, and of the holy Spirit, teaching them to observe all that I have commanded you. And behold, I am with you always, until the end of the age."

Matthew 28:18–20

CHAPTER 1

Passing On Faith

 **Have you ever been part of a relay race team?**
Each team member passes the baton to the next person in line, trying not to drop the baton. The race cannot continue unless one team member carefully passes the baton to the next. Just as we pass the baton to our teammate, Catholics take care to pass on our faith, although our faith is more precious than a baton. We pass on our faith by staying close to God and teaching others about our faith. This begins at Baptism, when we first become members of the Church. We commit to learn about the Church and to share what we learn with others. We pass on our faith.

Making Christians

A long time ago, just 200 years after Jesus ascended to Heaven, a Christian writer named Tertullian wrote that "Christians are made, not born." Tertullian was saying that the Church uses certain methods to make **Christians.** Tertullian's reminder was saying the same thing that Jesus said right before he ascended to Heaven:

> *"Go, therefore, and make disciples of all nations, baptizing them in the name of the Father, and of the Son, and of the holy Spirit, teaching them to observe all that I have commanded you."*
>
> (Matthew 28:19–20)

Jesus is telling us to go out and baptize and teach others what he taught us. He showed us through his own life that good Christians should be examples of faith, hope, love, forgiveness, compassion, mercy, and justice. We are called to show others how to be a follower of Jesus', a **disciple.** The word *disciple* comes from a Latin root word that means "to learn." We need to learn about our faith so that we can show others what it means to live as disciples.

> **Christians are made, not born.**
> [Tertullian, Church Father, Third Century AD]

 Think and Write

Write what the word *Christian* means to you.

_____

_____

_____

Looking Ahead

You are on a journey to being formed as a Catholic. So what does a Catholic look like? You have probably seen pictures or drawings of saints. All Catholics are called to become saints. **Saints** are holy, faithful people. But we don't have to perform miracles or do amazing things to be saints. The early Church called all the faithful followers of Jesus "the saints." And how did the saints live? The saints devoted themselves to holding on to their faith, expressing their faith, living their faith, and praying their faith.

> *"They followed the teachings of the apostles, they lived together, they celebrated the breaking of the bread, and they prayed."*
>
> (adapted from Acts of the Apostles 2:42)

The Four Pillars of Our Faith

Think about a sturdy wooden chair. What makes that chair sturdy? Each leg holds some of the weight of the seated person. Just like that sturdy chair, Catholics have four legs to stand on that help us live out and share our faith. The following are the four pillars of our faith:

1. the Creed

2. the sacraments

3. the moral life

4. prayer

The saints were the first followers of Jesus. They believed in these pillars and lived according to them. When we are baptized, we enter into a loving relationship with God and with others. These four pillars help us act as disciples in all that we do.

Facts of Our Faith: *The Nicene Creed*

We pray the **Nicene Creed** at Mass. It is based on the Creed developed by the Council of Nicea in A.D. 325. The Creed was given its final form in 381 at the Council of Constantinople. The Creed is a reflection of the unity of the members of the Trinity—God the Father, God the Son, and God the Holy Spirit. It is a reflection of the unity we are called to have with one another.

Friendship Example	The Catholic Faith
Think about how you treat a friend.	Our close and loving relationship with God and with one another is supported by:
1. You love your friend because you believe certain things about him or her to be true, such as your friend is kind or forgiving.	1. what we believe about God (the Creed).
2. You express your love for your friend, such as through hugs, sharing, or helping.	2. how we express our love for God and how God shows his love for us (the sacraments).
3. Your actions show your love and respect for your friend.	3. how we act toward God and toward others (the moral life).
4. You communicate with your friend.	4. how we communicate with God (prayer).

1. The Creed

Who are some people that you believe in? Why do you believe? To believe in someone is to have a relationship with that person and to trust that person. The trust that a baby has for his or her mother is a good example. The baby learns to trust because the mother changes diapers, feeds, bathes, and comforts the baby. The baby has faith in the mother because of the mother's loving actions.

Our faith in God is like that. The stories in the Bible show that God has always been faithful to his people. The stories of the saints are great examples of God's love and trust. People in our lives show us faith by sharing their own experiences. Our own life experiences can lead us to believe that God can be trusted. In the Creed, we say what we believe.

2. The Sacraments

Humans express their love in many ways other than words, such as smiles or kind actions. As Catholics, we worship at Mass and participate in the **sacraments.** We use signs, symbols, and rituals to experience God and to express our love for him. Sacraments are sacred signs of our faith and are instituted by Jesus Christ.

 Live It!

Just as the Sacrament of Baptism welcomes us into the Church, describe one way you can welcome someone new into your parish community.

_____

_____

_____

3. The Moral Life

Think about how you feel when you do something you know you shouldn't do. Think about how you feel when you do something thoughtful for someone for no reason. You might do it just to show someone that you care about him or her. God loves us. He is inviting us to love him and others. Because we love God, we are called to show that love. We try to avoid actions that don't show love. That is how we can live a moral life. It's that simple.

Living a moral life should be easy. There are only 10 rules to follow—the **commandments**—and God is so wonderful and loving, who would ever do something he would not like? The truth is that we can forget how good God is to us. This can lead to bad choices.

Living the moral life is not just avoiding bad things and choices. It is a matter of recognizing how God loves us and then responding to that love by loving our neighbors. God is faithful to us, and we cannot hurt God through our bad choices. We can only hurt ourselves.

 **Facts of Our Faith:**
The Commandments

The first three commandments teach us about loving God. The last seven commandments teach us about loving our neighbors.

Live It!

Write about one way you can show God's love to someone in need in your community.

_____

_____

_____

4. Prayer

How do we communicate with people we love? We talk and listen to them. Prayer is the best way to communicate with God. Communication is both speaking and listening. People sometimes forget to listen. If we don't listen, we are missing the voice of God. We will learn more about how God speaks to us and what it means to hear God's voice later in this book. For now, know that prayer is the fourth pillar of our Catholic faith. Without prayer, that sturdy chair would have only three legs, and it would collapse.

> If we don't listen, we are missing the voice of God.

Think and Write

Describe times when you talk to God and when you listen to God.

_____

_____

_____

_____

_____

So What?

So what difference does it make for Catholics to believe that "Christians are made, not born"? It means that we are called to respond to God by living our faith. If we follow the four pillars of our faith, we can be examples for others. Faith is something that we receive. It does not belong to us; it is passed on to us. We care for, protect, and pass on our faith. We can think of God as the potter and ourselves as the clay. God, through the Church, shapes us.

Review

Scripture

"Go and make disciples of all nations, baptizing them in the name of the Father, and of the Son, and of the Holy Spirit. Teach them to observe all that I have given you. Know that I am with you forever and always."   (adapted from Matthew 28:19–20)

Prayer

Lord God, each day is a new chance for you to make me into one of your disciples. Help me to stay close to you through prayer and to share your love with others. Amen.

Chapter Highlights

- "Christians are made, not born."
- We are called to be disciples.
- The four pillars of our faith are the Creed, the sacraments, the moral life, and prayer.

Terms to Remember

Christian   commandment   disciple   Nicene Creed   sacrament   saint

React

One way I can follow the Creed this week is:

_____

One way I can participate in the sacraments this week is:

_____

One way I can live out the moral life this week is:

_____

One way I can communicate with God through prayer this week is:

_____

At Home

Discuss this question with a grown-up. Write your answer.

Name a person you think is a role model of faith. What can we learn from him or her?

_____

_____

CHAPTER 2

God Calls, We Respond

 **What hobbies do you like to do?** Are you interested in making jewelry, doing science experiments, or building things? Why do you like it? When you finish a project, who sees it? Most people like to share their interests with others. When people get to know our interests, they get to know us. In the same way, God is very interested in his creation. We can get to know God better through his marvelous creation. God invites us to share and participate in his creation. God shows himself to us in many ways that remind us to stay close to him.

Getting to Know You

Think about how you feel on the first day of school. Are you a little nervous about making new friends? Are you hoping that you will know some of the people in your class? When you get to school, what is one of the first things the teacher does? Most teachers introduce themselves and the students to one another. Some teachers might lead you in games that help you get to know a little bit about one another.

These games are often called ice breakers. Ice breakers might ask people to share information about their families, pets, interests, sports, or hobbies. Sharing this information helps you form relationships with others. For example, once you know that Olivia likes to play soccer, you might decide you want to get to know her better.

Our Catholic faith is about relationship with God. God wants each of us to be close to him. To do this, God reveals, or makes himself known, to us. Even though God knows everything about us, he is always inviting us to be closer to him. We call this act of God's self-revealing **Revelation.**

Revelation is God showing himself to us so that we can be close to him. God is the one that is inviting us to be with him. We are just saying yes to his invitation. God calls us, and he wants us to answer his call.

> **God calls us, and he wants us to answer his call.**

 Think and Write

Imagine that God is calling you on the phone. Why do you think he is calling?

_____

_____

_____

 Facts of Our Faith: *Revelation in the Bible*

Revelation is the act of something or someone being revealed. In the Bible, Revelation refers to God's act of revealing himself and his saving plan for us. We believe that the most important part of God's Revelation is Jesus. In Jesus, the invisible God becomes visible, revealed.

God Is in Charge

Imagine this scene. After school, you and a few friends decide to play a game outside. Right away Emma lays down the rules and chooses her team. You are surprised at her take-charge attitude. Such an attitude can be a very good thing. However, a different approach is needed in our spiritual lives. Being more spiritual is letting God take charge. When we decide that we should pray more, be nicer to our little brothers and sisters, or help in our community, we are simply doing what God has planned for us.

The story of Adam and Eve is an example of people trying to take charge spiritually. Adam and Eve decided they could take charge and become godlike by eating the fruit of the tree of knowledge of good and evil. They got God's attention, but he was not happy with them. God sent Adam and Eve away from the garden.

> Since the moment of our birth, God has been following us, seeking us out, and inviting us to be close to him.

Let's take a look at people who responded to God's call instead of taking charge.

- Abraham and Sarah recognized that God was calling them to a new life, and they responded by leaving their home and moving to a strange land.
- Moses saw God's presence in a burning bush and responded to God's invitation to lead his people out of slavery.
- Mary responded to God's messenger, the angel Gabriel, by accepting God's invitation to become the mother of his Son.

All of these people answered God's call by saying yes. They heard what God said and respectfully accepted. The challenge for all people is to respond to God's invitation. Since the moment of our birth, God has been following us, seeking us out, and inviting us to be close to him. Understanding this is very important. We must keep learning to find ways to respond to God's call. God has already taken the first step.

Think and Write

In your own words, fill in the chart by describing God's call to Isaiah and to Simon and Andrew. Then describe how they responded.

	God's Call	His People's Response
Isaiah 6:1–13		
Mark 1:16–20		

Thy Will Be Done

Jesus' entire life paints a picture of how to respond to God. He was able to say yes to God in every situation. Even when he knew he was going to die on the cross, Jesus was able to say ". . . still, not my will but yours be done." (Luke 22:42) When we see that God is the one leading us and taking charge, we can see that our job is to figure out what he is asking us to do. Then we can respond as Jesus did, "thy will be done."

 ## Live It!

Think of someone who has heard God's call in his or her life and has said yes. Describe how that person responded to the call. Then write one way you can follow his or her example.

_____

_____

_____

_____

_____

_____

Facts of Our Faith: *The Lord's Prayer*

You probably recognize the words "thy will be done." They are part of the Lord's Prayer. Two versions of the Lord's Prayer are found in the Gospels. One is found in Matthew and one in Luke. Matthew's version is the one the Church uses at Mass. Jesus used this prayer when instructing his disciples on how to pray. (*Catechism of the Catholic Church* 2767)

Humility

When we understand that God reveals himself to us and wants us to know him, we realize that "it's not about us." It's about God and what God is doing in our lives. This kind of attitude shows **humility.** What is humility? Humility is recognizing that all our gifts and talents come from God. Saints are not people who draw attention to themselves—they draw attention to God. Here are a few examples of how the saints lived their lives for God.

- John the Baptist said, "He must increase; I must decrease." (John 3:30)
- Mary said, "My soul proclaims the greatness of the Lord. . ." (Luke 1:46)
- Saint Ignatius of Loyola taught people to do all things for the greater glory of God.

John the Baptist, Mary, and Saint Ignatius all lived lives with great humility. They recognized that God was revealing himself to them and responded by doing God's will.

 Live It!

Before the Last Supper, Jesus showed great humility as he washed the feet of the disciples (John 13:5–17). How can you show humility in each of these examples?

A grandmother in a retirement home:

_____

_____

A child who is standing alone on the playground:

_____

_____

 So What?

So what does Revelation mean to Catholics? It means that we should learn to pay attention to God's call and respond by saying yes. Saint Ignatius of Loyola said to "find God in all things." It sounds difficult, but it's quite simple. We can find God in a flower or a warm hug, and we can find God in difficult times too. When we feel left out, we can learn to remember always to include others. When we're bored, we can use this time to share with God what's on our mind. When we get in trouble, we can reflect and turn back to God. God wants our attention. We can respond with humility in our words and actions.

Review

Scripture

Moses was tending the flock of his father-in-law Jethro. While he was leading the flock across the desert, he came to Horeb, the mountain of God. An angel of the Lord appeared to him in fire flaming out of a bush. When the Lord saw him coming closer, God called out to him from the bush, "Moses! Moses!" He answered, "Here I am."   (adapted from Exodus 3:1–2,4)

Prayer

Lord, God, since before I was born, you have been longing to be close to me. Help me to recognize the many ways you reveal yourself to me and to recognize your call for me. Help me to respond to your invitation to love you by loving others. Give me the grace I need to pray the words "your will be done." Amen.

Chapter Highlights

- Our Catholic faith is about our relationship with God.
- Revelation is God showing himself to us.
- God calls and we answer that call.
- We show humility when we realize it's not about us; it's about what God is doing in our lives.

Terms to Remember

humility   **Revelation**

React

We learned that God is always revealing himself to us. Where do you find God? On a separate sheet of paper, make a word web with the word *Revelation* in the middle. Write at least five ways you find God in your own life.

At Home

Discuss these questions with a grown-up. Write your answers.

How is God revealing himself to our family? What can we do to answer his call?

_____

_____

_____

CHAPTER 3

Who's the Boss?
Scripture and Tradition

 What are some things that people always think go together? Perhaps you think of salt and pepper, soap and water, socks and shoes, or the sun and the moon. In our Catholic faith, there is one important pairing that leads and guides us. That pairing is Scripture and Tradition. Scripture is the written Word of God found in the Bible. Tradition is the handing down of the teaching of the apostles through the Church and with the guidance of the Holy Spirit. Scripture and Tradition are linked together to guide us in our journey of faith.

"Says Who?"

Think about how you feel when your older brother or sister tells you what to do. Your sister might say "Clean your room." What would your response be? You might say "Says who?" You would want to know why she is giving you orders. If she responds "Says Dad," you might want to clean your room because you know that you should do what your parents ask. Her answer tells you that your dad gave your sister authority to tell you.

So what does the word *authority* mean? Authority means "the right to give orders or make decisions" or "a person that can be trusted to give the right information or advice."

Jesus spoke with authority. Jesus gave instructions about how to live. Some people asked where Jesus was getting his authority. They were asking "Says who?" Jesus made it very clear where his authority came from.

> *"All power in heaven and on earth has been given to me."*   (Matthew 28:18)

Jesus speaks with the authority of God. Jesus then gives this authority to his Church when he told Peter that he would build his church upon him and gave him the keys of the kingdom (Matthew 16:18–19). When people are given the keys to something, it shows they have authority. Teachers have keys to their classrooms. Adults have keys to their homes. Some people want to know where our authority comes from. All authority comes from God.

Scripture and Tradition

For Catholics, God's Revelation is found in both Scripture and Tradition. Remember that Revelation is God showing himself to us. **Scripture** is the Bible. The Old Testament contains the holy writings of the people of Israel and the New Testament contains the holy writings of the Christians. The writings in the Bible are inspired by the Holy Spirit.

The word *Tradition* has a special meaning to Catholics. **Tradition,** with a capital T, describes how the Church understands, accepts, and lives out the message of the Gospel (what Jesus taught). Tradition means more than the customs and practices that Catholics have (that's *tradition* with a lowercase *t*), such as the lighting of the Advent wreath candles or abstaining from meat on Fridays during Lent. Tradition (with a capital T) means that parts of our faith cannot be abandoned and that are binding for Catholics. Examples of Traditions are our belief that Jesus is both human and divine, that we are loyal to the pope as the Vicar of Christ, and that we are committed to the Eucharist as the Real Presence of Christ and the center of Christian life. Just as the Scriptures came to be, Tradition was formed by the guidance of the Holy Spirit.

God continues to speak to us through the pope, the bishops, and the teachings of the Church, which make up a living Tradition. In this way, God's Word continues to speak to us today, addressing issues that didn't exist when the Bible was written, such as environmental issues. Scripture and Tradition are partners in helping us to understand and stay close to our Catholic faith.

Passing on the Message

The high point of God's Revelation is Jesus Christ. Jesus speaks and acts with authority because he is the Son of God. Jesus then gives his apostles the mission to carry on his work and sends his Holy Spirit to guide them. In the Church, the bishops are the ones who make sure the message to Catholics remains faithful to the Gospel. They do this with the help of the Holy Spirit. The Word of God comes from both Scripture and a living Tradition. We can see how authority works with this diagram.

Facts of Our Faith:
The Magisterium

When talking about the teaching authority of the Church, we use the term **Magisterium,** referring to the bishops in communion with the pope and under the guidance of the Holy Spirit. We trust the Magisterium to authentically teach and interpret the truths of our faith, the Tradition. Read more about this on page 25.

| God has all authority. | → | God has given all authority to his Son, Jesus Christ. | → | Jesus has given authority to the Church, through Peter and his successors (the bishops). |

Live It!

We are called to act as disciples of Christ and teach others about Scripture and Tradition. Imagine you were explaining Scripture and Tradition to a younger student. Write a short explanation of each.

My explanation of Scripture is: _____

_____

My explanation of Tradition is: _____

_____

Which Came First—Scripture or Tradition?

The Bible, as we know it today, was formed by Church Tradition. People preached the Gospel before the New Testament was written. It began as oral tradition, people telling one another. Later, the leaders of the early Church put the books of the Bible in order. The Bible is the revealed Word of God. Here is some basic information about the Bible.

> **The Bible is the revealed Word of God.**

- The Catholic Bible is made up of 73 books: 46 books in the Old Testament and 27 books in the New Testament.
- The Old Testament is the story of the people of Israel before the birth of Jesus. The Old Testament begins with the Pentateuch—the first five books that tell the story of the relationship between God and his people. The other books include historical books about judges and kings. The Wisdom books and books about the prophets like Isaiah and Jeremiah complete the Old Testament.
- The New Testament is the story of the Christian experience. It begins with the life of Jesus Christ told in the Gospels of Matthew, Mark, Luke, and John. The Acts of the Apostles comes next and is followed by letters, known as the Epistles. The New Testament ends with the Book of Revelation.

 Live It!

Explore a Bible and read one Scripture passage. After reading, write the citation and describe what you thought about the passage.

_____

_____

 Think and Write

Scripture and Tradition are linked together. Fill in each link with one example you know about Scripture and Tradition.

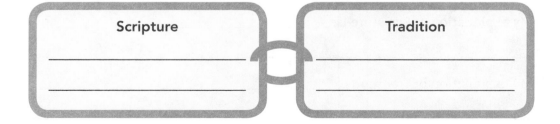

Scripture

Tradition

How Do Catholics Understand the Bible?

Catholics believe that everything in the Bible is true, but not necessarily fact. This points out that truth and fact are not always the same things. We can say that it is "raining cats and dogs" to tell a truth without using facts. We call this figurative language. It may be true that it is raining hard, but the fact is that it is not raining cats and dogs. There are parts of the Bible that rely on figurative language to show God's truth, such as in the parables.

Tradition and Decision Making

When Catholics are seeking guidance from God's Word, we can turn to the Bible. We also can look to Church Tradition. The Magisterium, the teaching authority of the Church, lets us look to what the Church, under the guidance of the Holy Spirit, has taught through teachings from our bishops and popes. The Magisterium includes writings from councils, letters from popes and the bishops, and the *Catechism of the Catholic Church*.

 Think and Write

Think about a difficult decision you have to make. How might you use Scripture and Tradition (the teachings of the Church) to help you decide what to do?

_____

_____

_____

_____

_____

 **Facts of Our Faith: Catechism of the Catholic Church**

The *Catechism of the Catholic Church* is a book to help us better understand more of what we believe. It is organized into four parts that mirror the four pillars of our faith: creed, sacraments, moral life, and prayer.

 So What?

So what difference does it make that Catholics believe that the sources of God's Revelation are Scripture and Tradition? Through Scripture and Tradition, we experience God's presence and the guidance of the Holy Spirit.

Review

Scripture

Be faithful to what you have learned and believed, because you know from whom you learned it. Since you were born you have known the sacred scriptures, which can give you wisdom for salvation through faith in Christ Jesus. All scripture is inspired by God and is useful for teaching and correcting, so that one who belongs to God may be able to do good work.

(adapted from 2 Timothy 3:14–17)

Prayer

Holy Spirit, guide us to see the Living God, revealed to us in Scripture and Tradition. Help us to receive God's Word and to be fed by it so that we may pass it along to others. Amen.

Chapter Highlights

- God reveals himself to us through both Scripture and Tradition.
- The Magisterium is the teaching office of the Church and helps us understand Tradition.
- When we have decisions to make, we can look for help from God's written Word and a living Tradition.

Terms to Remember

Magisterium   **Scripture**   **Tradition**

React

Write an example of tradition and Tradition.

_____

_____

At Home

Discuss this question with a grown-up. Write your answer.

Think of a problem in the world today. How can we use Scripture and Tradition to help find a way to solve this problem?

_____

_____

_____

CHAPTER 4

The Trinity

 **What do you see when you look in the mirror?**

Do you have your father's nose? Do you have your grandmother's eyes? People can tell that we are part of our family by the way we resemble our family—the way we look or the way we act is like someone else in our family. Besides being part of our family at home, we also belong to our Catholic faith family. And just like we may resemble our family at home, we can resemble God our Father—not in how we look but in how we act.

In the first book of the Bible, the Book of Genesis tells us that God created us, male and female, in the divine image. Being created in the image of God means that we have characteristics or personality traits that are god-like. So what is our image, or picture, of God? How do we "resemble" God?

You Look Familiar . . .

How do you feel when someone who knows your family says "You must be a Smith" or "You must be a Rodriguez"? It is good to feel proud of being part of our family. Besides our families at home, we are connected to our Catholic faith family. We are also associated with another name—the Trinity. The Creed, the first pillar of our faith, says that we believe in God who is Father, Son, and Holy Spirit. What this means is that the Christian image of God is seen as one God in three Persons. This is called the **Trinity.**

When we are baptized, the priest blesses us with the words "In the name of the Father, and of the Son, and of the Holy Spirit." When we pray the Sign of the Cross, we are reminded of the Trinity. In this prayer, we pray to God our Father, who creates all things because he loves us. We pray to the Son, Jesus, who came to tell us of the Father's love and to save us. We pray to the Holy Spirit who helps us to understand how much God loves us and to help us show God's love to others. The Trinity is like our family name.

Facts of Our Faith: *The Sign of the Cross*

At Confirmation, the bishop seals us with the Sign of the Cross on our foreheads with holy Chrism. Each time we pray the Sign of the Cross, we can recall this seal. It stresses our belief in the Trinity. The use of holy water when we make this sign recalls our Baptism. The Sign of the Cross is a visible sign of what we believe.

We believe in God who is Father, Son, and Holy Spirit.

Think and Write

Think about some personality traits that might describe God—the Father, Son, and Holy Spirit. Use words to describe your image of God.

My image of God is:

_____

_____

_____

_____

_____

Live It!

Choose one of the traits you used to describe your image of God. How can you use this trait to show others that you are made in the image of God?

_____

_____

_____

_____

The Trinity Is a Mystery

What do butterflies emerging from their chrysalis and stars that shoot across the sky have in common? They're mysterious to us. We can see these mysteries, but we may not fully know how they happen. In faith, mystery is something that can be known, or believed in, even if we don't fully understand it. The Trinity is a mystery. We can know in our hearts that God is the Father, Son, and Holy Spirit who calls us to a deeper love that we can share with one another.

When we reflect on God as Father, Son, and Holy Spirit, we recognize that God is a community of love. God does not keep this love, but shares it with all of us. This is why love of neighbor is so important in Christianity. We reflect the image of God when we love our neighbors. Love for others is not just a trait of God's, but is the very heart of God.

> When we reflect on God as Father, Son, and Holy Spirit, we recognize that God is a community of love.

What does this all mean? It means that the Trinity—the Father, Son, and Holy Spirit in a loving relationship—is the most perfect image of who God is and how God is present and active in the world. Because we are made in the image and likeness of God and baptized in the name of the Father, Son, and Holy Spirit, we are to be in a loving relationship with one another and with God.

The Church as Community

What does *community* mean to you? What do you picture when you hear the word?

A **community** is a group of people living together or gathering together because of a similar interest. It's a relationship with others. Your neighborhood is a community. The baseball league is a community. A recycling club at school is a community.

The Church is God's community. As a member of this community, God asks us to help others see him present and active in our daily lives. When you go to Mass, you will see parish members praying and singing together as one community. The priest, ushers, lectors, and musicians at church work together to help celebrate Mass. The Church community also works together to help others in need, such as collecting canned goods for those who are homeless or hungry. Together we work to serve others as Jesus did. We are called to be in communion, in relationship, with the world around us. We show others how we participate in the life of the Trinity through our words and actions.

As part of this Church community, we are called to speak out against things that prevent people from living in loving relationships with one another. One way to do this is by accepting all our classmates as equals. Another way is helping out with a food drive at school. These actions help others see the Trinity at work. This honors our family name. We are part of a community based on that loving relationship. When we are baptized in the name of the Father, Son, and Holy Spirit, God calls us to live life in unity, or **solidarity,** with others. We reflect the image of the Trinity—communion and love.

> We show others how we participate in the life of the Trinity through our words and actions.

We believe in the Trinity as a relationship. God the Father, the Creator of all things loves us; God the Son, Jesus, saved us from our sins and loves us; and God the Holy Spirit loves us, blesses us, and supports us. If you know you are loved by God, then you *know* the Trinity.

Think and Write

Name two communities to which you belong. Write a sentence that describes the interest or goals of each community. Then tell how each community might be an example of God's love.

_____

_____

_____

_____

Live It!

Whenever we offer our love to others, we are sharing in the life of the Trinity. Write one example of this love that you see in your Church community.

_____

_____

_____

_____

So What?

So what difference does it make that Catholics believe in the Trinity? It means that we believe that God is in loving relationship with us, and, because we are made in the image of God, it is our nature to live in loving relationship with one another. To live in loving relationship with others is to share in the divine life of the Trinity. This also means that we have a name to live up to, just like we have to live up to our family name. Since we are baptized in the name of the Father, and of the Son, and of the Holy Spirit, we need to live up to the name of God—the Holy Trinity.

Facts of Our Faith: *Solidarity*

The Trinity's love for us is the model of our love for one another. God calls us to be in solidarity with all people. Solidarity means that we see that we are all part of the same human family no matter what country we live in, what race we are, or what religion we practice. The Gospel calls us to be peacemakers. We are called to love our neighbors and promote peace in the face of the problems in our world.

Review

Scripture

After Jesus was baptized, he came up from the water. Suddenly the heavens were opened. He saw the Spirit of God descending like a dove and coming upon him. A voice came from the heavens, saying, "This is my beloved Son, with whom I am well pleased."

(adapted from Matthew 3:16–17)

Prayer

Glory be to the Father, and to the Son, and to the Holy Spirit, as it was in the beginning, is now and ever shall be, world without end. Amen.

Chapter Highlights

- We believe in the Trinity—one God, three Persons.
- God the Father, God the Son, and God the Holy Spirit is a community of love.
- As members of the Church community, God asks us to help others see him—Father, Son, and Holy Spirit—present and active in our daily lives.

Terms to Remember

community   **solidarity**   **Trinity**

React

How do you recognize each Person of the Trinity working in your own life?

_____

_____

At Home

Discuss these questions with a grown-up. Write your answer.

What can we do to show people who are living in poverty that we are in solidarity with them? Why do you think God calls us to live in solidarity with one another?

_____

_____

_____

CHAPTER 5

Sin, Salvation, and the Cross of Jesus

What do books such as *Charlotte's Web* and *Old Yeller* have in common with movies such as *Up* and *The Incredibles*? Besides being interesting, fear and death are important parts of their themes. Fear is a normal human emotion. The Bible talks about people's fears, such as the fear of death. As Catholics, we know that Jesus Christ conquered death. Jesus gives us new life through his Resurrection and Ascension. Our new life begins at Baptism when we are given new life through Jesus Christ. We are now part of Jesus' community of love and are called to share this new life with others.

A Choice That Changed Everything

Have you heard about Adam and Eve? The story in the Book of Genesis tells us that God gave Adam and Eve a beautiful garden to live in and a special gift. He told them they could eat from any tree in the garden except one. He gave them the ability to choose between right and wrong. That ability is called **free will**. God wanted Adam and Eve to choose love and life with him. Instead, Adam and Eve chose to eat the fruit from the forbidden tree. This choice brought a kind of darkness and death into the world. People would become fearful and continue to make choices that separated them from God. Sometimes we make choices that offend God. When we make these choices, we **sin**.

 Live It!

Think about a situation in which someone you know might be making a bad choice. How would you encourage that person to choose to do what is right?

_____

_____

_____

 **Facts of Our Faith:**
Original Sin

Adam and Eve represent all people. Because of Original Sin, humans choose to follow what we want instead of following God's will. In Baptism, Original Sin is "washed away." This is because Jesus became man, died, rose, and ascended into Heaven. Jesus' Death and Resurrection save us from sin and give us new life.

Jesus Saves Us

When Jesus became man, he became just like us. He had hopes, dreams, and fears. Like us, Jesus faced temptation. Unlike us, Jesus never gave in to temptation. He did not sin. Jesus faced suffering and death. He was an innocent victim. He was put on a cross to die in public. He was treated like a criminal. However, Jesus did not lose his battle with sin and death. God raised Jesus up from the dead. Jesus, through his **Resurrection**, overcame death and sin. We know now that death is not the end. We are saved because even death cannot separate us from the love of Jesus Christ.

Jesus's life, Death, and Resurrection are summed up in a section of the Nicene Creed. We pray:

For us men and for our salvation
he came down from heaven,
and by the Holy Spirit was incarnate of the Virgin Mary,
and became man.

For our sake he was crucified under Pontius Pilate,
he suffered death and was buried,
and rose again on the third day
in accordance with the Scriptures.

As baptized followers of Jesus, we still face sin and temptation, suffering, and death. But, through Jesus, we know that we can overcome all of these things.

 Think and Write

Think about what you know about the life, Death, and Resurrection of Jesus. Write what you know under each heading in the chart.

Jesus Lived	Jesus Died	Jesus Rose

The Cross—Our Trophy

Trophies are signs for certain accomplishments. We may get trophies for winning a basketball game, spelling bee, or science fair. Trophies are signs of victories. We can look at the cross as a sign of victory. Just as a winning team marches in a parade, lifting up the trophy for all to see, we Catholics march in parades. We call them processions. Processions are led by the Cross of Jesus, lifted up for all to see. The message is loud and clear: if Jesus can overcome suffering and death, then we, through Baptism, can overcome anything.

The Cross and Challenges

People of faith—people who can see that God can and will win over everything—need to share this knowledge with those who are sad or suffering. This is why we, as Catholics, visit those who are sick, elderly, lonely, and others who are in need of love and care. We do not try to convince them of God's presence, or to ignore their pain and suffering. We show God's continuing care for them through our loving presence.

> **The message is loud and clear: if Jesus can overcome suffering and death, then we, through Baptism, can overcome anything.**

 Facts of Our Faith: *Stations of the Cross*

One of our faith traditions is to recall the Death and Resurrection of Jesus, using Stations of the Cross. Praying them helps us to express our love for God. Many churches have crosses or illustrations to show each station. There are 14 stations that represent events from Jesus' Passion and Death. Some versions include a 15th station showing the Resurrection. We use our imagination to reflect on Jesus' suffering, Death, and Resurrection. There are many different ways the Stations of the Cross are depicted, but they all remind us of what Jesus did for us. Learn more about the stations on page 137.

Live It!

Think about one person who may be sad or is suffering from an illness. Tell how you can show God's love for that person through your actions.

_____

_____

_____

_____

The Gift of Salvation

Where and with whom do you feel safe? Most of us feel safe with our parents and other family members. We feel safe at home or in other familiar places. With Jesus, we are always safe. Through Jesus, we are saved. Because we are saved, we share in eternal life. We no longer see death as the end, but as a change. **Salvation** in Jesus is a gift. The only way to experience Salvation is to know the suffering, Death, and Resurrection of Jesus. This means that we always try to avoid sin and to live as a true follower of Jesus'. We do good works in response to this great gift. Having faith in Jesus gives us a future and a new life.

> **With Jesus, we are always safe.**

Think and Write

Think about what Jesus did for you by dying on the cross. Write a note to thank Jesus for this gift of Salvation.

_____

_____

_____

So What?

So what difference does it make that Catholics believe in the Cross of Jesus? The fact that Jesus conquered death is the source of all of our hope. We have nothing to fear because nothing—not even death—can separate us from the greatest gift of all: the love of God in Christ Jesus.

Review

Scripture

I am convinced that nothing can separate us from the love of God in Christ Jesus our Lord.

(adapted from Romans 8:38–39)

Prayer

Lord, God, help me to live without fear. Help me to see that Jesus understands my greatest challenges and my greatest fears. Teach me to turn to him to make good choices in all that I do. Amen.

Chapter Highlights

- Jesus, through his Resurrection, overcame death and sin.
- Salvation is a gift.
- Nothing can separate us from the greatest gift of all: the love of God in Christ Jesus.

Terms to Remember

free will   Resurrection   Salvation   sin

React

Write a poem that describes how we receive new life through the life, Death, and Resurrection of Jesus.

_____

_____

_____

At Home

Discuss this question with a grown-up. Write your answer.

Why do you think people are afraid of death?

_____

_____

_____

_____

CHAPTER 6

The Church, Mary, the Saints, and Eternity

What team sports do you like to play? What is similar about teams for baseball, basketball, soccer, and volleyball? Teamwork is very important. Each player has to do his or her best so that the players can count on one another. Being part of your church community works the same way. You can count on people in your parish, Mary, and the saints to support you. And you should do your best to support others in your church community.

More Than Just a Slice of the Pie

Clubs bring people together. We might think that belonging to the Church can be compared to belonging to a club, like Boy Scouts, Girl Scouts, or the chess club.

> **The Church is the living Body of Christ.**

Not really. We really don't *belong* to the Church. We actually *become* the Church. The Church is not a club. As easily as you join a club, you can quit. This may sound a little like Church, but here's the difference. The Church is the living Body of Christ. Just like our hands, feet, arms, and legs are all part of our body, we are joined to the Body of Christ. Through Baptism, we are joined to the Church in a very important way. As the Body of Christ, we are joined to one another and to Christ with our heart, mind, and soul. We are connected with one another and with Christ.

 Think and Write

Each wedge of the pie shows a daily activity. Fill in the amount of time you think you spend on each one. What does your pie look like? Where do you spend most of your time? How much of your pie do you think should be pray or worship?

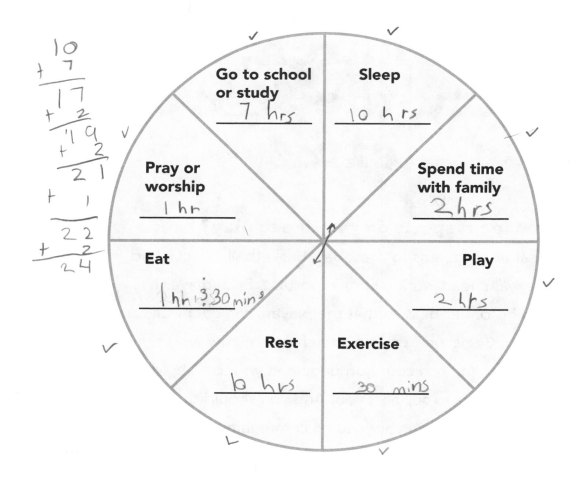

10
+ 7
——
17
+ 2
——
19
+ 2
——
21
+ 1
——
22
+ 2
——
24

Go to school or study   7 hrs

Sleep   10 hrs

Pray or worship   1 hr

Spend time with family   2 hrs

Eat   1 hr : 30 mins

Play   2 hrs

Rest   6 hrs

Exercise   30 mins

Think about paying attention to God in our thoughts and actions. Our spiritual life is not a slice of the pie at all. It is the whole pie! In Baptism, we become the Church. We are part of the divine life of Jesus. This means that everything we do should be connected to Jesus.

Just like a star player on a soccer team might think she can take the ball down the field and score the winning goal on her own, sometimes we think we can do things without Jesus. As the soccer player forgets the importance of teamwork, we forget the importance of the Body of Christ and the Trinity. We need to recognize that God is always present in our lives. As members of the Church, we honor God everywhere and in everyone. Baptism does not make us members of an exclusive club; it makes us members of the living Body of Christ.

Stewardship

Family members spend time together, teach one another about things they like to do, such as sports, hobbies, and games, and share what they own. The Church works the same way. When we share as the Church, we are practicing stewardship. **Stewardship** is the sharing of our time, talent, and treasure. Treasure is more than money and possessions. It's anything we value. One of the keys to being more spiritual is learning to recognize the presence of God in all things, in all people, and in all situations. Then we can respond to God by sharing our time, talent, and treasure.

> **We need to recognize that God is always present in our lives.**

Live It!

Write one way you can share your time, talent, and treasure.

Time _____

_____

Talent _____

_____

Treasure _____

_____

The Marks of the Church

We all have characteristics that make us different from one another. Eye or hair color, the ability to play an instrument, and freckles all give us our own special identity. There are marks that help identify the Church. The **Marks of the Church** are that the Church is one, holy, catholic, and apostolic.

> . . . the Church is one, holy, catholic, and apostolic.

one The word *one* points out the unity, or oneness, of Christ's Church. The Church is one just like the Trinity—God the Father, God the Son, and God the Holy Spirit are one.

holy God alone is holy. This is a way to say that God is God and we are not. As members of the Church, we are called to share in God's holiness by showing others his love.

catholic Catholic with a capital C means "the Roman Catholic Church." When we say "I believe in one, holy, catholic, and apostolic church," **catholic** means "universal," and a lowercase c is used. We are saying that Christ's Church invites all to belong.

apostolic We know that God has all authority and that he gave his authority to Jesus. We also know that Jesus passed on his authority to the Church through Peter and the apostles. The Church still follows the teaching of the apostles. The pope, who is the bishop of Rome, and the bishops, priests, and deacons lead the Church (all who are baptized) to pass on the teachings of the apostles from generation to generation. By handing down the teaching of the apostles, the Church is **apostolic**.

So when we say "I believe in one, holy, catholic, and apostolic church," we are saying that we believe in a Church that trusts in the Trinity, has divine roots and guidance, is open to all people, and is faithful to the teachings of the apostles. These things make the Church very easy to recognize.

Facts of Our Faith: *Pentecost*

Jesus told Simon, "You are Peter, and upon this rock I will build my church" (Matthew 16:18). The Acts of the Apostles 2:1–13 tells us how 50 days after his Resurrection and 10 days after he ascended into Heaven, Jesus sent the Holy Spirit to the apostles. This event is called the Feast of Pentecost. We can think of Pentecost as the birthday of the Church.

Think and Write

Fill in each room of the church below with pictures and captions to show what you know about the Marks of the Church.

| one | holy |
| catholic | apostolic |

Models of Faith—Mary and the Saints

How do babies learn to walk or talk? They learn by imitating the people they see every day. In fact, all living creatures learn by imitation. If we want to grow spiritually, we look to others to show us how to follow Jesus. The people we can learn from are usually those closest to us: parents, older brothers and sisters, godparents, grandparents, and close friends. The Church also gives us role models who have followed Jesus by living lives of holiness. These people are the saints. By learning about the lives of the saints, we can learn how to answer God's call in our own lives.

Facts of Our Faith:
The Rosary

The Rosary is a devotional prayer that recalls events in Mary's and Jesus' lives. Learn about the Rosary on pages 134–136.

The greatest example of all the saints is Mary, the mother of Jesus. Mary holds a special place of honor for Catholics. Mary said yes to God's will by being the mother of God's only Son. We honor Mary by calling her the Mother of God and the Mother of the Church. Just as we go to our own mothers when we need help and guidance, we can go to Mary. We can ask her to help us grow closer to her son, Jesus. By following Mary's example and with her help, we can become more faithful disciples.

The Church celebrates Mary on five special days. Each day reminds us of some important events in her life.

Immaculate Conception: On December 8, we celebrate that Mary was free from Original Sin.

Presentation of Mary: On November 21, we recall from a traditional story that Mary's parents brought her to the Temple when she was three years old to present her to the Lord.

Annunciation: On March 25, we remember that the angel Gabriel announced to Mary that she is to be the mother of the Son of God.

Visitation: On May 31, we celebrate the day that Mary, pregnant with Jesus, visited her relative Elizabeth, who was pregnant with John the Baptist.

Assumption: On August 15, we celebrate the day that Mary was taken up to Heaven at the end of her earthly life.

For centuries, people have looked to the saints as examples of holiness and faithfulness. As with Mary, we honor the saints. We do not worship them. Worship is for God alone. When we pray before statues or pictures of saints, we are asking them to help us grow closer to Jesus. Statues, icons, medals, and other sacred images help us to focus our prayer.

The Communion of Saints and Life Everlasting

Heaven is when we are fully in the presence of God—Father, Son, and Holy Spirit. Hell is when we are completely separated from God after death. God does not send us to Hell. Hell is "chosen" by people who reject God's love and mercy. **Purgatory** is when those who die love God, but who have not fully let go of things that separate them from God's love. Before we enter into God's presence in Heaven, we must be free from sin. We pray for those in Purgatory so that they may be united with God in Heaven.

Just like we stay in touch with those who are far away, we can pray to people who make up the Communion of Saints. The **Communion of Saints** is made up of saints and all who faithfully followed Jesus in their lives but have passed from this life into the next. These can be parents, grandparents, children, and neighbors. We can pray for them, and they can pray for us.

Facts of Our Faith:
Salvation Outside the Church

What about Protestants, Muslims, Hindus, Buddhists, Jews, and other non-Catholics? The Church teaches that every person who is saved, even those outside the Church, is saved by Jesus Christ in ways only known to God. So non-Catholics who seek God with a sincere heart and try to do God's will as they understand it are still in communion with the Church in a different way and can be saved.

Live It!

Think of a saint or a person you knew who has died. Write a prayer asking him or her to help you show others how to live as part of the Church.

_____

_____

So What?

So what difference does it make that Catholics believe in the Church, Mary, the saints, and eternity? The Church is the vehicle that carries us on the path to Jesus. We are bound to one another and driven by hope and love. Mary and the saints are role models who help us live with hope and teach us how to follow Jesus. They are part of the Communion of Saints, and we can ask for their help. In Jesus, we have been given a glimpse of eternal life. In the risen Christ, we know what waits for us if we follow him.

Review

Scripture

Then I saw a new heaven and a new earth. The old heaven and earth had passed away, and the sea was gone. I also saw the holy city, a new Jerusalem, coming down out of heaven from God. I heard a loud voice from the throne saying, "Behold, God's home is with the human race. He will live with them and they will be his people. God himself will always be with them. He will wipe every tear from their eyes, and there shall be no more death or mourning, wailing or pain, for the old order has passed away."   (adapted from Revelation 21:1–4)

Prayer

God the Father, Son, and Holy Spirit, thank you for inviting me to share in your divine life as a member of your Church. Help me to learn from the example of Mary and the saints, to follow Jesus more closely, and to do what you want me to do with the help of the Holy Spirit. Amen.

Chapter Highlights

- The Church is one, holy, catholic, and apostolic.
- Mary and the saints are examples of how to follow Jesus.
- We believe in eternal life given to us through Jesus.

Terms to Remember

apostolic	Communion of Saints	Purgatory
catholic	Marks of the Church	stewardship

React

How can you be a model of your faith?

_____

_____

_____

At Home

Discuss this question with a grown-up. Write your answer.

How can we show others that we truly believe that the Church is catholic?

_____

_____

_____

PART 2

The Sacraments: Expressing Faith

For I received from the Lord what I also handed on to you, that the Lord Jesus, on the night he was handed over, took bread, and, after he had given thanks, broke it and said, "This is my body that is for you. Do this in remembrance of me." In the same way also the cup, after supper, saying, "This cup is the new covenant in my blood. Do this, as often as you drink it, in remembrance of me." For as often as you eat this bread and drink the cup, you proclaim the death of the Lord until he comes.

1 Corinthians 11:23–26

CHAPTER 7

Worship and Liturgy

 **Not so long ago you were in kindergarten.** One of the first things you were taught may have been to stay in line as your class walked through school. You may have had a line leader each day. Staying in line showed that you knew how to follow directions and work together. Our Catholic faith is like a line leader. It helps us to "line up" with God and to be united with him. As Catholics, we do this through worship and liturgy.

Aligning Ourselves with God

Has your bike ever had a crooked wheel? To be safe, we need to be sure that our bike tires are aligned properly. On our own journey of faith, we have to learn to align ourselves with what God wants for us. Our Baptism is the first step in aligning ourselves with God. It doesn't matter if we celebrated our Baptism as a baby or just recently. To live our Baptism each day means that we try to align ourselves with God's will in all that we do.

As Catholics, we try to align with God in many ways, including through worship. Some words that might help you understand worship are *praise, honor, glory, adoration, thanksgiving,* and *devotion.* Any way in which we align ourselves with God is a way to **worship** him.

When we worship with the other members of our parish, we call our worship **liturgy.** The most important liturgy we practice is the celebration of the Mass, but the Church celebrates other liturgies as well. They include celebrating the sacraments and the Liturgy of the Hours. The sacraments are the center of the liturgy of the Church. They help us move toward Christ and align ourselves with God. All liturgy celebrates the Paschal Mystery of Christ—his suffering, Death, and Resurrection. When we celebrate the liturgy, we experience God's grace and are changed.

 **Facts of Our Faith:** *The Liturgy of the Hours*

The Liturgy of the Hours is the daily public prayer of the Church. With this practice, we praise God and recognize that the entire day is holy. It begins with a morning prayer of praise (Lauds), continues with daytime prayer, an evening prayer (Vespers), and night prayer (Compline).

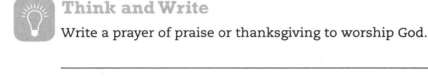 **Think and Write**

Write a prayer of praise or thanksgiving to worship God.

_____

_____

_____

The Sacraments of the Church

Stops signs, traffic lights, exit signs, and street signs help guide drivers on the road. The sacraments are signs to guide us on our faith journey. They are signs that reveal God's presence and bring his grace into our lives. Jesus established the sacraments and gave them to the Church. The Church has seven sacraments. When we celebrate the sacraments, we worship God and grow in holiness as individuals and as a community. The sacraments can be grouped together in the following way:

Sacraments of Initiation: Baptism, Confirmation, and the Eucharist

Sacraments of Healing: Penance and Reconciliation, and the Anointing of the Sick

Sacraments at the Service of Communion: Holy Orders and Matrimony

 Think and Write

Describe what you know about these sacraments, including the signs and symbols.

Baptism _____

_____

Confirmation _____

_____

Eucharist _____

_____

Penance and Reconciliation _____

_____

Anointing of the Sick _____

_____

Holy Orders _____

_____

Matrimony _____

_____

Who? How? When? Where?

Who celebrates the sacraments? The Church, the entire Body of Christ under the inspiration of the Holy Spirit, celebrates the sacraments.

How do we celebrate? We use many signs, symbols, and rituals. We read from Scripture. We walk in procession. We sing. We bow, kneel, stand, and sit. We combine word and action to make visible the invisible grace of Christ. Beyond the church walls, we continue to worship God by loving others and showing others grace through our actions.

When do we celebrate? During the liturgical year, with Easter at its center, we celebrate the Paschal Mystery of Jesus through different seasons and feasts. Throughout the liturgical year, we can also celebrate the sacraments and honor Mary and the saints. Every day we can pray the Liturgy of the Hours with the whole Church.

> We combine word and action to make visible the invisible grace of Christ.

Where do we celebrate? Although we can and do pray anywhere, the Church dedicates certain spaces as sacred. Church buildings provide us with these sacred spaces that remind us of the significance of what takes place when we worship Almighty God.

Live It!

The Church's celebration of sacraments involves certain rites and rituals. Many families have their own ways to celebrate when family members receive the sacraments. How might you celebrate a sacrament, such as First Holy Communion, with your family and friends before and after the church celebration?

_____

_____

_____

_____

The Liturgical Year

Your family probably has a calendar at home to keep track of important events, such as birthdays and dentist appointments. The Church uses a calendar called the **liturgical calendar.** This highlights the seasons and feasts in the Church year. The liturgical calendar represents the celebration of the mystery of Christ. It starts with the anticipation of his birth and continues through his Death, Resurrection, and Ascension. It then moves to the expectation of his return. The Church marks the passage of time with a cycle of seasons and feasts that invites us to deepen our relationship with Jesus. The liturgical calendar represents the celebration of the mystery of Christ.

Advent is the beginning of the Church year. It begins four Sundays before Christmas. Advent is a season of hope and joy in which we prepare to celebrate the birth of Jesus and to anticipate his second coming.

The **Christmas** season starts with Christmas, the celebration of Jesus' birth. This is followed by the **Epiphany,** when Jesus became known to the world. The season ends with the Feast of the Baptism of Our Lord.

Ordinary Time is the time for celebrating our call to follow Jesus as his disciples day by day. The Sundays of the entire year are counted as sacred time. Ordinary Time (typically 33 weeks) is celebrated after the Christmas season and again after Easter.

Lent begins on Ash Wednesday. It is a time of turning toward God in preparation for Easter. Throughout these 40 days, the whole Church prepares by praying, fasting, and giving alms. Alms are gifts for someone in need.

Holy Week recalls the events surrounding the suffering and Death of Jesus. This week begins with Jesus' entrance into Jerusalem on Palm Sunday and ends on Holy Saturday with the vigil of his Resurrection. We celebrate the high point of the liturgical year by marking the **Triduum**, our "Passover" celebration of Jesus' Death and Resurrection.

 Facts of Our Faith: *Triduum*

The Easter Triduum is the three days before Easter. It begins on Holy Thursday evening with the Mass of the Lord's Supper. We remember how Jesus showed the disciples his love by washing their feet. The Triduum includes Good Friday and Holy Saturday. On Good Friday, there is no Mass, but people pray the Stations of the Cross and hold a service that recalls the Passion, the time between the Last Supper and the moment Jesus dies on the cross. During this service, we honor the Cross of Jesus. Holy Saturday is a day of prayer and reflection. The Triduum ends with the Easter Vigil Mass after sundown.

Easter celebrates Jesus being raised from the dead. Because the Resurrection is the central mystery of the Christian faith, the Church sets aside 50 days of joyful celebration. These days, from Easter to Pentecost, are celebrated as one feast day, sometimes called "the great Sunday." Easter is celebrated on the first Sunday after the first full moon of spring.

Pentecost is the day on which we celebrate the coming of the Holy Spirit upon the disciples 50 days after Jesus' Resurrection. With this feast, the Easter season ends. Pentecost is our celebration of the "birthday of the universal Church."

> **Pentecost is our celebration of the "birthday of the universal Church."**

Live It!

What are some ways you can share the peace of Christ with others through prayer and almsgiving during Lent and throughout the Church year?

_____

_____

_____

_____

_____

So What?

So what difference does it make that Catholics worship? It means that we continually align ourselves with God's will. Without worship, we sometimes do things that prevent us from loving God and neighbors. To worship is to love and direct all our attention to God. The sacraments are visible signs of God's invisible grace. The sacraments help us to move toward Christ and align ourselves with God.

Review

Scripture

Shout joyfully to the Lord, all you lands; / serve the Lord with gladness; / come before him with joyful song. (Psalm 100:1–2)

Prayer

Lord, God, I sometimes find it hard to focus my attention on you. Help me to align myself with your will. Help me to worship you and to recognize what you ask me to do. Amen.

Chapter Highlights

- We align ourselves with God through worship and liturgy.
- We worship as the Church through liturgy.
- The sacraments are outward signs of God's grace.
- The liturgical calendar represents the celebration of the mystery of Christ.

Terms to Remember

Advent	Epiphany	liturgical calendar	Pentecost
Christmas	Holy Week	liturgy	Triduum
Easter	Lent	Ordinary Time	worship

React

What are two ways you worship with your family?

_____

_____

At Home

Discuss this question with a grown-up. Write your answer.

What can we do as a family to put more focus on worship throughout each week?

_____

_____

CHAPTER 8

Mystery and Sacramentality

 Think of how you celebrate birthdays, Christmas, or other special days with your family and friends. On these days, people show that they care for us in many ways. Maybe your grandmother sends a card or your parents or friends give gifts. These actions are signs that make us feel loved by others. Signs can say something to us that words alone do not. Sometimes God speaks to us by using signs. We can grow closer to God through the signs of our Catholic faith that help us know the mystery of God.

It's a Mystery

When we know someone loves us, we can think of signs of that love in our life. We have learned that God has revealed himself to us in the same way and continues to reveal himself to us now. We can be sure God loves us through reading his story in the Bible and experiencing his presence in the sacraments.

In the Catholic faith, the central mysteries through which God reveals himself to us are the Paschal Mystery and the Trinity. These ways also let us experience his love. At Mass, we are invited to proclaim the mystery of our faith. We are proclaiming our belief in the **Paschal Mystery** of Christ: that through Jesus' suffering, Death, and Resurrection, we have new life. The word *paschal* comes from the Greek word for *Passover*. Passover is the time when the Jewish people celebrate the night their ancestors were saved from the angel of death. They brushed a lamb's blood on the doorposts of their homes. We are saved from sin by the blood of the Lamb of God, Jesus. He is our Passover, our Paschal Mystery. This mystery is at the heart of our faith: from death comes new life.

> In the Catholic faith, the central mysteries through which God reveals himself to us are the Paschal Mystery and the Trinity.

We have learned that God is Father, Son, and Holy Spirit. In the Paschal Mystery, we discover how God the Father sent his Son, Jesus, to pass through death to new life in the Resurrection. Jesus did this to save us from our sins.

 Facts of Our Faith: *Consecration*

The Consecration of the Eucharist—the bread and wine changing into the Body and Blood of Christ—takes place during the Eucharistic Prayer. It is the point in Mass when the risen Jesus Christ becomes physically present on the altar so that we may receive him at Holy Communion.

Mystery of Our Faith

The mysteries we are discussing here are neither puzzles nor detective mysteries to be solved. They are about God's love for us that is so great we will never understand it completely. Answer the questions below to explore the mystery of our faith.

Who is God?

_____

_____

How do we get to know God?

_____

_____

Clues we can use:

_____

_____

_____

What are the big mysteries?

_____

_____

What do we know about them?

_____

_____

Think and Write

In what ways is the mystery of God's love revealed to us?

_____

_____

_____

Live It!

What things can we do to show others how much God loves us?

_____

_____

All Catholics Know Sign Language

What do teachers do to get students to pay attention in class? Some teachers clap three times. Others count down from five to one. Still others use hand signals. These are good ways to get attention. We Catholics also use signs in our worship and liturgy. These signs help us show our relationship to one another and to God. We use words and actions to express ourselves to God. Praying the Sign of the Cross, tracing the cross on our foreheads, lips, and chest, and extending our hands with palms up are all gestures we use to show our connection with God. We use signs because words alone are not enough.

We use many signs, symbols, rituals, and gestures to show our connection with God. Catholics believe that God can be found in all things. So when we celebrate our encounters with God in the seven sacraments, we use ordinary things from the natural world. We use water, fire, oil, bread, and wine as visible signs.

> **Catholics believe that God can be found in all things.**

In our prayers and devotions, we can use pictures and sacramentals to help us in our prayer. **Sacramentals** are blessings, gestures like the Sign of the Cross, statues, holy cards, rosaries, crucifixes, and other sacred images. Sacramentals help us draw our attention to God. Statues of Mary or the saints remind us of God's grace and presence in the world. Sacramentals can also be used to teach about God, Scripture, and the history of the Church.

In the Bible, God used many signs to reveal his presence. He spoke to Moses from a burning bush. He sent manna from the sky to feed his people. He led the Israelites through the desert with a pillar of fire and columns of smoke. God

> God used signs, symbols, and rituals, along with words, to teach.

used signs, symbols, and rituals, along with words, to teach. These things were all part of God's language. The Catholic Church is a faith of sacraments and sacramentals that worships by using a language beyond words, just as God did in the past and still does today.

Think and Write

Choose two sacramentals that are in your home or a friend's home. Describe them and tell how they are used.

_____

_____

Live It!

There are many troubling events in the world today. Write a prayer intention for a cause. Then come together as a group to pray aloud using a sacramental to focus your prayer.

_____

_____

_____

_____

So What?

So what difference does it make that Catholics understand and believe in the Paschal Mystery? It means that we understand that Jesus died, he is risen, and he will come again. This mystery is the center of our faith: from death comes new life. Catholics worship by using signs, symbols, and rituals. When we worship, we use the same language God uses. We use a language beyond words. Just as we learned to speak from our parents, we learn to speak the language of God from our Father in Heaven.

Review

Scripture

Then King Darius wrote to all the people on earth: "All peace to you! Throughout my royal domain, the God of Daniel is to be reverenced and feared: 'For he is the living God, and will be forever; his kingdom shall not be destroyed, and his power shall be without end. He is a deliverer and savior, working signs and wonders in heaven and on earth, and he delivered Daniel from the lions' power.'"   (adapted from Daniel 6:26–29)

Prayer

Lord, God, you have revealed yourself through signs and wonders. This is your language. Help me to see the signs and wonders all around me. Help me to feel your presence and hear your voice in the celebration of the sacraments. Amen.

Chapter Highlights

- The Paschal Mystery is that Jesus died, is risen, and will come again.
- We will never totally understand the mystery of how much God loves us.
- The Catholic faith is a sacramental faith.
- We use signs, symbols, and rituals to express our faith.

Terms to Remember

Paschal Mystery   **sacramental**

React

Explain how sacramentals are part of the language of our faith.

_____

_____

_____

At Home

Discuss this question with a grown-up. Write your answer.

How can we explain to someone who is not Catholic why gestures, symbols, signs, and rituals are important in our faith?

_____

_____

CHAPTER 9

Sacraments of Initiation

 Have you ever worked with clay? You can shape and mold clay into almost anything. You can make a soap dish, a pencil holder, or a sculpture. The best thing about working with clay is that if you are not happy with what you have made, you can reshape it to make something new. God shapes us and molds us as well. The Church helps with this shaping and molding, forming, and re-forming through Baptism, Confirmation, and the Eucharist. These sacraments are called the Sacraments of Initiation.

Sacraments That Welcome Us

Think about how it feels to be a member of a group. You might be a Girl Scout, a Boy Scout, or play on a hockey team. Some groups have ceremonies to welcome you to the group. The Catholic Church has three special ceremonies that welcome us at different times in our lives and continue to strengthen us as Church members. These are the **Sacraments of Initiation.** These sacraments are Baptism, Confirmation, and Eucharist. God reshapes and re-forms us with these special celebrations. He continues to mold us and shape us throughout our lives.

- **Baptism** is our entrance into new life in Jesus' Church.
- **Confirmation** seals us with the Holy Spirit. The Holy Spirit helps us share what we know about Jesus with others.
- In the **Eucharist,** we receive the Body and Blood of Jesus Christ, which makes us one with him.

> **The Catholic Church has three special ceremonies that welcome us at different times in our lives and continue to strengthen us as Church members.**

Baptism

Catholics often use the word *rite* to describe a sacramental celebration. During the Rite of Baptism, there are gestures and words that help us understand the richness of the sacrament. Dressed in white, the person being baptized is signed with the Sign of the Cross and hears the proclamation of the Word of God. Then he or she is anointed with both the oil of catechumens and Chrism. The oil of catechumens symbolizes the strengthening of the person preparing for Baptism. The sacred Chrism symbolizes sharing Christ's ministry. The person being baptized is also given a baptismal candle, which is lit from the Easter candle. These signs, gestures, and words proclaim the faith into which the person is being baptized.

Baptism frees us from Original Sin, the sin we are all born with, and gives us new life. We become members of our Church community and part of the Body of Christ. The signs of Baptism are water, oil, white garments, and light. Baptism can be done at any age, but it is never repeated. Once you are baptized, you are a member of the Church forever.

Think and Write

Write an acrostic poem using the letters of the word *Baptism* as the first letter of each line. Tell what you know about Baptism in your poem.

B _____

A _____

P _____

T _____

I _____

S _____

M _____

Confirmation

Throughout Scripture, the Holy Spirit is described by using images such as wind, breath, fire, and a dove. These are signs for the Holy Spirit. The Holy Spirit is the third Person of the Trinity who calls us into a deeper relationship with Jesus Christ and the Father. This relationship is established and reinforced through Baptism and Confirmation.

> **The Holy Spirit is the third Person of the Trinity.**

What are the signs that help us recognize the presence of the Holy Spirit during Confirmation? Let's take a look.

- **Laying on of hands**—The bishop extends his hands over those to be confirmed. He calls on the Holy Spirit to share the seven Gifts of the Spirit with us.
- **Anointing with the sacred Chrism**—The bishop anoints the forehead of those being confirmed and says "Be sealed with the Gift of the Holy Spirit."
- **The bishop**—The bishop himself is a sign that shows us the presence of the Holy Spirit in the Church, going all the way back to the apostles.

Confirmation strengthens our relationship with God. We are called to lead holy lives as disciples dedicated to God and the mission of the Church. The signs of Confirmation are the laying on of hands and anointing with sacred Chrism. Confirmation can only be received once, just like Baptism.

The Gifts of the Holy Spirit

In the Sacrament of Confirmation, we receive these seven gifts.

Wisdom—seeing the importance of keeping God as the center of our lives

Understanding—understanding the meaning of God's message

Knowledge—thinking about and exploring God's Revelation, and also recognizing that there are mysteries of faith beyond us

Fortitude—having the courage to do what one knows is right

Counsel—seeing the best way to follow God's plan and making good choices

Piety—praying to God

Fear of the Lord—an attitude of reverence before God who is always with us and whose friendship we do not want to lose

How Do We Recognize the Holy Spirit?

Do you believe in wind? Most likely, you do. Have you ever seen the wind? No. Wind is invisible. But we can see what wind does. We can see leaves blowing, branches bending, and waves in the ocean. In a similar way, we can recognize the presence of the Holy Spirit by the influence or effects the Spirit has on people. We call these effects the Fruits of the Holy Spirit.

love	joy	peace	modesty
patience	kindness	goodness	self-control
generosity	gentleness	faithfulness	chastity

Think and Write

How do you see the Holy Spirit working in people you know? Write about a time when you saw someone demonstrate a fruit of the Holy Spirit.

_____

_____

_____

Live It!

Choose two different Fruits of the Holy Spirit listed on page 66. Then tell how you can show others the presence of the Spirit in you. For example, you can show patience when teaching your brother to catch a baseball.

_____

_____

_____

Eucharist: Our Family Meal

What are family meals like in your home? Family meals are opportunities for people to eat and share. Meals are a celebration of family love. The food helps fuel our bodies. The conversation keeps us connected with one another. The Mass, the celebration of the Eucharist, is like a family meal. The Mass is the central celebration of parish worship. As part of God's family, the Body of Christ, we remember Jesus' sacrifice. He becomes present to us in the Eucharist, and we share Holy Communion with our Church family.

> The Mass is the central celebration of parish worship.

Every Sunday, when we receive Holy Communion, we are reminded that God loves us and gives us strength to face all of life's challenges. For Catholics, receiving Holy Communion is the ultimate acknowledgment that God is our source for everything that we need.

The Mass

The Mass follows a pattern that includes the following parts:

Introductory Rites: The Mass begins with rites that help us get ready to hear God's Word and receive Jesus Christ in Holy Communion.

Entrance Chant: The Entrance Chant's procession, led by the cross, represents our movement toward the altar of God.

Penitential Act: This includes a prayer of sorrow for sins and a petition, or request, for God's mercy.

Gloria: a hymn of praise, which is not sung during Advent or Lent

Collect Prayer: This prayer points out our reason for coming together to celebrate and asks God for his grace.

Liturgy of the Word: We hear the story of God's plan for Salvation in readings from the Old and New Testaments proclaimed from a book called the *Lectionary for Mass.*

First Reading: generally from the Old Testament

Responsorial Psalm: from the Psalms

Second Reading: generally from one of the New Testament letters

Gospel Reading: a proclamation of the Good News of Jesus from one of the four Gospels (Matthew, Mark, Luke, or John)

Homily: The priest or deacon helps us understand how to relate our lives to God's Word.

Profession of Faith: We express our faith and trust in God—the Father, Son, and Holy Spirit—and in the Church.

Prayer of the Faithful: We offer prayers for our needs and the needs of the world.

Liturgy of the Eucharist: We gather around the altar to prepare the sacred meal of the Eucharist.

Presentation and Preparation of the Gifts: A chalice (for the wine) and a paten (for the host) are placed on the altar. Members of the assembly, those gathered to worship, carry bread, wine, and water to the altar.

Prayer over the Offerings: During this prayer, the priest prays that our sacrifice may be acceptable to God.

Eucharistic Prayer: The prayer begins with the Preface—a song of praise to God—and the Holy, Holy, Holy. The most important part of the Eucharistic Prayer is the Consecration, through which the bread and wine truly become the Body and Blood of the risen Christ. At the end of the Eucharistic Prayer, the priest holds up the host and chalice and sings a song of praise (the Concluding Doxology) to the Trinity. The assembly responds with a resounding "Amen."

Communion Rite: The Communion Rite includes The Lord's Prayer, the Sign of Peace, the Lamb of God, and the assembly receiving Holy Communion. After a short period of silence to give thanks, the Communion Rite ends with the Prayer after Communion.

Concluding Rites: The Concluding Rites include the Dismissal. The priest or deacon encourages us to go out and live our mission as Christians.

There are many signs and symbols in the Mass. As Catholics, we use signs, symbols, and gestures to express our faith. The signs of the Eucharist are unleavened bread and wine. The Sacrament of the Eucharist is the only Sacrament of Initiation that we receive over and over again. In fact, the Church encourages us to receive Holy Communion as often as we can.

Facts of Our Faith: *Real Presence*

The Eucharist is the Real Presence of Jesus Christ under the appearance of bread and wine. The Council of Trent (A.D. 1545–1564) declared that after the Consecration of bread and wine, Jesus Christ is really and truly present in the Eucharist. In Saint John's Gospel, Jesus asserts that he is the Bread of Life, the true bread come down from Heaven for the life of the world (John 6:48–51).

Live It!

If possible, as a group or with your own family, attend a daily Mass. Write about how daily Mass was the same as or different from Sunday Mass. Tell how you felt going to a daily Mass.

_____

_____

_____

Think and Write

How is a family meal like the celebration of the Eucharist?

_____

_____

_____

A Different Path to Holiness

Many members of the Church receive Baptism as infants, First Holy Communion as young children, and Confirmation as preteens or teenagers. But the Church has another process of Initiation to prepare and welcome adults and children of catechetical age, usually seven, to the Church. It is called the Rite of Christian Initiation for Adults (RCIA). The RCIA is a period of reflection and instruction for those wishing to become Catholic. The RCIA takes place over many months or even longer. The RCIA members are welcomed into the Church during the Easter Vigil Mass. The RCIA process prepares people to be disciples of Jesus united with their Church community.

 Facts of Our Faith: *Reunited—Sometimes!*

In the early Church, Baptism and Confirmation were celebrated at the same time. Now they are often separated by many years. This change happened when Christianity became the official religion of the Roman Empire and the number of people wishing to be baptized was greatly increased. The bishops were not able to be present at every Baptism, so they allowed priests to perform Baptism, but not Confirmation. The Second Vatican Council recognized the unity of the two sacraments and allowed pastors to confirm RCIA participants at the Easter Vigil.

So What?

So what difference does it make that Catholics believe in and celebrate the Sacraments of Initiation? It means that we can be re-formed and shaped into the image of Christ. In celebrating these sacraments, we are formed into followers of Jesus Christ and brought into unity with him and the Church. Through Baptism, our sins are forgiven, and through Confirmation, we are sealed with the Holy Spirit. In the Eucharist— the Real Presence of Jesus—we find strength for our journey. In the Sacraments of Initiation, we are reshaped by God, the master potter, to be more like Jesus in all that we do. This pattern of re-forming and reshaping will continue the rest of our lives.

Review

Scripture

Keep, then, this custom of the unleavened bread. Since it was on this very day that I brought your people out of the land of Egypt, you must celebrate this day throughout your generations as a permanent tradition.

(adapted from Exodus 12:17)

Prayer

Loving God, through Baptism, you take away sin. Holy Spirit, in Confirmation, you guide us along the path and help us to be faithful. Lord, Jesus Christ, you feed us through the Eucharist so that we may continue the journey. Holy Trinity, thank you for these sacraments. Amen.

Chapter Highlights

- The Sacraments of Initiation are Baptism, Confirmation, and the Eucharist.
- These sacraments re-form and reshape us into followers of Jesus Christ, his disciples.
- For Catholics, the Eucharist is the Real Presence of Jesus Christ.
- At Mass, we remember Jesus' life, Death, and Resurrection.

Terms to Remember

Baptism   **Confirmation**   **Eucharist**   **rite**

React

Describe how those who experience the Sacraments of Initiation are changed.

Sacrament	How are we changed?
Baptism	
Confirmation	
Eucharist	

At Home

Discuss this question with a grown-up. Write your answer.

As a family, how can we make Sunday different from every other day of the week?

_____

_____

CHAPTER 10

Sacraments of Healing

 **Have you ever had an argument with a brother, a sister, or a friend?** What do your parents ask you to do when that happens? They might ask you to say "I'm sorry. I realize that I was wrong." Your parents might also tell you to shake hands or hug each other. God knows us and knows that we are not perfect, so he gave us a sacrament to help us when we sin. That sacrament is called the Sacrament of Penance and Reconciliation. We can think of this sacrament as a way to say "I'm sorry" to God. In turn, God reminds us how much he loves us by "washing away" our sins.

The Sacrament of Penance and Reconciliation

Have you ever watched babies who are just learning how to walk? They stand up but they are still a little wobbly. Usually they take two or three steps and fall down. What do they do next? Do they just give up and go back to crawling? They pick themselves up and try again. Babies never give up trying to learn to walk. When it comes to sin, we have to have that same attitude. God recognizes that all humans are not perfect. He is always willing to forgive us and show us his mercy, but we have to recognize our sins and ask for forgiveness. Jesus has given us a gift to show us his mercy. It is the Sacrament of Penance and Reconciliation.

Think about how you feel when you make a bad choice. Sin separates us from God and from others. God is always calling us back to him when we sin. We are given new life at Baptism. As we continue our faith journey, we are invited to renew our Baptism through the Sacrament of Penance and Reconciliation. Each time we receive this sacrament, we experience God's forgiveness and mercy. This helps us grow closer to Jesus and to learn to be more like him when we face choices that tempt us to sin.

> **God is always calling us back to him when we sin.**

In the Sacrament of Penance and Reconciliation, going to a priest, confessing our sins, and hearing the words of forgiveness are ways we can experience forgiveness from our sins. This sacrament heals and restores our relationship with God and with our community. We can receive this sacrament as often as we want.

The signs of Penance and Reconciliation are the words we use and the words the priest uses. We must be truly sorry for our sins, confess them to a priest, and be willing to fix what we have done. When we do these things, we experience God's healing mercy and forgiveness.

 Think and Write

Why do we go to a priest to confess our sins?

Because our priest can give forgivness through the sacrament, Penance, and Reconciliation.

The Liturgy of Reconciliation

Before we receive the Sacrament of Penance and Reconciliation, we need to think about things we might need to confess. An **examination of conscience** is the act of looking prayerfully into our hearts to ask how we have hurt our relationships with God and with other people. We reflect on the Ten Commandments and the teachings of the Church. When celebrating this sacrament, the priest and the person confessing his or her sins follow these steps:

1. We receive a greeting and blessing from the priest.

2. The priest may read from Scripture. (optional)

3. We confess our sins.

4. The priest gives us **penance,** usually prayers to pray or an act to do, to complete.

5. We pray an Act of Contrition.

6. The priest prays that God will forgive us, and the priest gives us absolution.

7. We praise God for forgiving us.

8. The priest dismisses us.

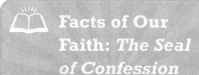

Facts of Our Faith: *The Seal of Confession*

In the Sacrament of Penance and Reconciliation, the priest must not tell anyone else about the sins that people confess to him. The person confessing his or her sins must be treated with dignity and respect. This confidentiality is called the "sacramental seal." (*Catechism of the Catholic Church* 1467)

The Four "-tions" of Reconciliation

The Sacrament of Penance and Reconciliation includes the following:

- Contrition—We examine our conscience by asking ourselves how we may have hurt our relationship with God and with others. We say we are sorry for our sins, and we promise to try not to repeat the same sins.
- Confession—We name the sins aloud to the priest.
- Absolution—The priest forgives our sins through the words of absolution.
- Satisfaction—We try to repair the damage our sins have caused by doing our penance.

Think and Write

Write some words that you or the priest might say during each part of the reconciliation process.

Facts of Our Faith: *What's with All the Names?*

So what's with all the names for the sacrament in which Jesus forgives sins?

- Reconciliation
- Penance
- Penance and Reconciliation
- Confession

These names all refer to the same experience of receiving forgiveness of our sins through confession to a priest. The *Catechism of the Catholic Church* calls this sacrament the Sacrament of Penance and Reconciliation—so that's its official name. (*Catechism of the Catholic Church* 1440)

Contrition: _____

_____

Confession: _____

_____

Absolution: _____

_____

Satisfaction: _____

_____

We try to repair the damage our sins have caused by doing our penance.

Live It!

Draw a comic strip showing how it might look to ask for forgiveness from a friend.

First

Next

Then

Finally

The Anointing of the Sick

If someone in your family is sick, what do you do to help? We can pray for them, make sure they have what they need, and keep them company. These things can help them feel better. In our faith, we know that prayer and spirituality can also help with healing. There are many stories in the Bible about Jesus' healing. These healings were signs of how God was working in the world. Through another sacrament of healing, the Anointing of the Sick, we celebrate God's presence through healing, compassion, and mercy.

Through the Sacrament of the Anointing of the Sick, Jesus becomes present to us to help us heal. Jesus shows us his compassion and mercy, lifts our hearts, and fills us with confidence, trust, and hope. This spiritual healing can help with physical healing as well because our spiritual and physical selves are connected. Through the Anointing of the Sick, we realize that Jesus is with us and that we have nothing to fear.

Who Is This Sacrament For?

If you have a cold, you don't need this sacrament. Although you might not feel very well, it is not a serious illness. This sacrament is for anyone suffering from a serious illness. Those to be anointed may include the following:

- a person preparing for surgery
- someone who suffers from the weakness of old age
- children or adults who are seriously ill
- people with chronic illness or addictions
- people suffering from serious mental health problems

This sacrament may be repeated if the sick person recovers after being anointed and becomes ill again or if during the illness the patient gets worse. The sign of this sacrament is the holy oil used to anoint the hands and head of the person who is sick.

The Liturgy of the Anointing of the Sick

In the past, the Anointing of the Sick was considered private and was done with just the priest and the sick person. Today, the Church celebrates the fact that we are all part of the Church community and encourages family and friends to be present for the ritual. The ritual includes the following:

- a penitential rite—we call to mind our sins.
- Liturgy of the Word—we listen to God's Word.
- laying on of hands—the priest lays his hands on the head of the sick person.
- anointing with the Oil of the Sick—the priest anoints the forehead and hands of the sick person and says "Through this holy anointing may the Lord in his love and mercy help you with the grace of the Holy Spirit. May the Lord who frees you from sin save you and raise you up."
- viaticum—for those who are close to dying, the priest offers the Sacrament of Penance and Reconciliation and the Eucharist. The Eucharist that is given to someone close to dying is called **viaticum,** which means "food for the journey."

The Sacraments of Healing are signs that we continue the ministry of healing that Jesus began. We follow his example of mercy, healing, and forgiveness.

> **The Sacraments of Healing are signs that we continue the ministry of healing that Jesus began.**

Think and Write

Think about a situation in which a person might need the Anointing of the Sick. Write why you think that person might wish to receive this sacrament.

_____

_____

_____

_____

Live It!

Write the words you would use if you sent a get-well card to someone who is sick in your parish.

So What?

So what difference does it make that Catholics receive the Sacraments of Healing? The Sacraments of Healing offer an opportunity to grow closer to God, to learn from our mistakes, and to bring us back to our relationship with God.

Review

Scripture

The Pharisees and their scribes complained to his disciples, saying, "Why do you eat and drink with tax collectors and sinners?" Jesus said to them in reply, "Those who are healthy do not need a physician, but the sick do. I have not come to call the righteous to repentance but sinners."

(Luke 5:30–32)

Prayer

Lord, Jesus, you are the healer of my soul, my body, and my spirit. Forgive my sins and fill me with your grace. When I'm sick, use your healing hand and restore me to health. Lord, may all who are sick and suffering experience your healing touch. Amen.

Chapter Highlights

- The Sacraments of Healing are the Sacrament of Penance and Reconciliation and the Anointing of the Sick.
- We believe that telling our sins aloud to a priest and hearing the words of forgiveness are part of the healing process.
- These sacraments continue the healing ministry of Jesus.

Terms to Remember

examination of conscience   **penance**   **viaticum**

React

Explain how the steps in the Sacrament of Penance and Reconciliation help us have a closer relationship with God.

_____

_____

_____

At Home

Discuss these questions with a grown-up. Write your answers.

What sins do we see in the world today? How can we show others how important it is to avoid these sins?

_____

_____

_____

CHAPTER 11

Sacraments at the Service of Communion

When families go to a restaurant, they want to be served a nice meal. It's a night off for the whole family. No one has to cook, set the table, or clean up after dinner. The waitperson has one job—to serve the diners. As Catholics and members of the Body of Christ, we are also called to serve. Some people serve as husband and wife, mother and father, in marriage. Others serve the Church as priests, deacons, and bishops. The sacraments that show the call to service in these specific ways are called the Sacraments at the Service of Communion. They are the Sacrament of Matrimony and the Sacrament of Holy Orders.

It's Not About Us

At Baptism, we become members of the Body of Christ. Our faith teaches us to put others before ourselves. As members of the Church and part of a faith family, we are asked to live as part of a community. We are called to help one another and serve one another since the day we became part of God's family, the day we were baptized.

> We are called to help one another and serve one another since the day we became part of God's family, the day we were baptized.

This commitment to help and serve one another is reinforced with the Sacraments of Matrimony and Holy Orders. These sacraments are vocations. A **vocation** is our life's work, our mission, and our purpose. The mission of these sacraments is to serve the Kingdom of God. These vocations show others the selfless love that all baptized Christians are called to share. This is why they are called the Sacraments at the Service of Communion.

The Sacrament of Holy Orders

Men who receive Holy Orders help continue Jesus' presence on earth in the tradition of the apostles. The Sacrament of Holy Orders is made up of three different levels, or hierarchies.

A **bishop** is the head of a local church or diocese. He is also part of the episcopal college, which is all the bishops of the world and the pope. Bishops may preside at all the sacraments. Only bishops may ordain priests. Bishops usually celebrate Confirmation unless the bishop gives a priest the authority to celebrate it.

Some bishops receive an honorary title of cardinal, which means that together, as the college of cardinals, they serve as special advisors to the pope. Cardinals under the age of 80 are also eligible to participate in a papal conclave, the process to elect a new pope.

A **priest** serves the community in many ways. Priests preside at liturgies. They preach, administer sacraments, counsel people, serve as pastors of a parish, and teach.

A **deacon** participates in the ministry of the bishop by serving the needs of the community. Deacons may proclaim the Gospel, preach, teach, baptize, witness marriages, and assist priests at liturgies. Some deacons are preparing to become priests. Others will remain deacons for life. These deacons may be married.

The Liturgy of Ordination

The rites of ordination for bishops, priests, and deacons use these words and actions:

The imposition of hands—The bishop imposes, or places, his hands on the heads of those being ordained.

The words of consecration—The bishop asks God to send the Holy Spirit and his gifts to those being ordained.

✓ **Anointing with oil**—Bishops are anointed with oil that is poured on their heads, while priests are anointed with oil on their hands.

The sign of Holy Orders is the laying on of hands.

 Facts of Our Faith:
The Episcopal College

The episcopal college is a group that is modeled after the twelve disciples. Jesus chose the disciples and made Peter the head of the group. Today, the pope, just like Peter, is the leader, and the bishops are just like the other apostles. The bishop's main task, along with the priests, is "to preach the Gospel of God to all men." (*CCC 881–888*)

 Think and Write

Write how your priest helps your parish.

Your Church Leaders

Who is the leader of the entire Roman Catholic Church? The pope is the leader of the Church. The bishop is the leader of your diocese, and a pastor is the leader of your parish. All of these leaders dedicate their lives to serving the Church. They help spread the good news of the Gospel and are examples of how to live a life of holiness.

Live It!

Fill in the names of your church leaders. Then choose one person and write a note to thank him for his work.

Pope: _Francis_

Name of your diocese: _Chicago_

Your Bishop: _Blase Joseph Church_

Name of your parish: _St. Gilbert_

Your pastor and priests: _Father John Chrzon_

Deacons in your parish: _Tom Biegel, Brian Fisher,_
and Mark Plaiss.

Thank You _____

_____
_____
_____
_____
_____
_____

Facts of Our Faith: *A Bishop's Symbols*

There are traditional symbols that represent a bishop's office. A bishop holds a crosier, which is the pastoral staff to symbolize a shepherd. The miter is a head covering that symbolizes the kingship of Christ and the bishop's connection with the pope. The bishop wears a pectoral cross on a chain around his neck to show that Christ is close to his heart. The bishop also wears a gold ring on the third finger of his right hand that symbolizes a bishop's close relationship with the people of his diocese.

The Sacrament of Matrimony

Matrimony, or marriage, is another example of our baptismal call to serve others. The man and woman have a deep love and a lifelong commitment to each other and the children they bring into the world. This love is a living sign of the love that God has for all of us. Marriage reminds all who are baptized that we are called to love and serve one another. Marriage is a **covenant** modeled after Christ's love for the Church. In marriage, a man and a woman become united—they become one.

The man and the woman entering into marriage actually give each other the sacrament by agreeing to marry in the presence of the priest (who serves as a minister of the Church), two witnesses, and the congregation. The marriage is a sign of God's love for the world to see.

> **Marriage reminds all who are baptized that we are all called to love and serve one another.**

The people in a marriage are called to love each other as Jesus loves all of us. These words of Jesus from the Gospel of John reinforce the importance of love in the Sacrament of Matrimony.

> *This is my commandment: love one another as I love you. No one has greater love than this, to lay down one's life for one's friends.* (John 15:12–13)

At the time, Jesus was speaking to his disciples, but these words apply to marriage also. The married couple promises to love and honor each other. They promise to take care of each other and to stay together until they are parted through death. They live out their vocation by loving each other and their children and by teaching their children about the faith. With this sacrament, they form a covenant with each other and with God. The Holy Spirit is the source of love and strengthens their love.

The Liturgy of Marriage

The most important part of the Rite of Marriage is that the couple consents to be married in the presence of a minister of the Church (a priest or deacon), two witnesses, and the congregation.

The priest or deacon invites the couple to offer their consent, saying, "Since it is your intention to enter into marriage, join your right hands and declare your consent before God and his Church." The couple then publicly states their consent, which is also symbolized by the blessing and exchanging of rings. Catholics are encouraged to celebrate their marriage within the Eucharistic liturgy, although they are not required to do so.

The signs of marriage are the husband and wife and their public expression of consent, which is further symbolized when they exchange rings.

The Domestic Church

The family is often called the domestic church. The family is where children learn to worship God, to love, to forgive, and to work together. Parents teach their children about the Catholic faith. The Holy Spirit guides the family to pray together, to worship together, and to share their love and the love of God.

Facts of Our Faith:
Communities of Prayer

We form a community of prayer when we gather together to celebrate Sunday Mass. A family forms a community of prayer when it prays grace before and after meals.

Think and Write

How can you show others that you are living your role as part of your family—the domestic church? I promise to make my family

a place of prayer by:

_____

a loving community by:

_____

a serving community by:

_____

a forgiving community by:

_____

Live It!

Men and women who marry use their gifts and talents to serve family life. Bishops, priests, and deacons serve the Church, families, and communities. What are your special gifts? How do you think you might use them to serve God and help others?

_____

_____

So What?

So what difference does it make that Catholics celebrate the Sacraments of Holy Orders and Matrimony? It means that we recognize that it's not about me! These two sacraments are called Sacraments at the Service of Communion. They remind us that we are all called to put the needs of others before our own needs.

Review

Scripture

But Jesus called the disciples to listen to him and said, "Whoever wishes to be great among you will be your servant; whoever wishes to be first among you will be your slave. I did not come to be served but to serve and give my life for many."   (adapted from Matthew 20:25–28)

Prayer

Lord, Jesus, you teach us not to serve ourselves, but to serve God and others. Help me to focus not on my own needs, but on the needs of others. Bless our Church, Lord, with good priests and strong marriages so that together we may build our community of faith. Amen.

Chapter Highlights

- The Sacraments of Service are the Sacrament of Matrimony and the Sacrament of Holy Orders.
- These sacraments reinforce our baptismal call to serve others.
- Matrimony and Holy Orders are both vocations.

Terms to Remember

bishop	**deacon**	**priest**
covenant	**Matrimony**	**vocation**

React

Write examples of why you think Matrimony and Holy Orders are Sacraments of Service.

Matrimony _____

_____

Holy Orders _____

_____

At Home

Discuss this question with a grown-up. Write your answer.

What can we do as a family to show that we are living out our baptismal call to serve others?

_____

_____

PART 3

The Moral Life: Living Faith

"You are the salt of the earth. But if salt loses its taste, with what can it be seasoned? It is no longer good for anything but to be thrown out and trampled underfoot. You are the light of the world. A city set on a mountain cannot be hidden. Nor do they light a lamp and then put it under a bushel basket; it is set on a lampstand, where it gives light to all in the house. Just so, your light must shine before others, that they may see your good deeds and glorify your heavenly Father."

Matthew 5:13–16

CHAPTER 12

Human Dignity, Sin, and Mercy

 **Think about how a student who just moved into town feels on the first day of school.** She doesn't know where her classes are, what to expect in the lunchroom, or if the other students will welcome her. Her clothes may be a little different. She sits quietly through the first few hours, but now you see her sitting all alone at a table in the back of the lunchroom. How do you think she feels? What would God expect you to do in this situation? The choice is yours. When we treat people kindly, we are showing God's love and care. The idea of treating all people with dignity and respect is at the heart of our faith.

All Equal in the Eyes of God

In Jesus' parable of the Last Judgment (Matthew 25:31–46), the king sits upon his throne in Heaven and meets all who have died. Those who helped others when they were hungry, thirsty, sick, or homeless; welcomed strangers; and visited those in prison are given eternal life. Those who ignored people in need were not given eternal life. The king says they should have recognized him in all people, including those suffering. If we do not realize that we are to treat all people as we would treat Jesus, our king, we are not acting as God calls us to act.

God calls us to act with morality. This means God expects us to make a **moral choice** between doing what is right and what is wrong. Making moral choices means recognizing the presence of God in people we meet so that we treat each person with respect. We are to consider the feelings of another person and not judge them by how they look or how they live. The Book of Genesis teaches us that God creates us in his image.

> *God created mankind in his image; in the image of God he created them; male and female he created them.*
>
> (Genesis 1:27)

People sometimes forget about the divine in one another. So God sent his only Son, Jesus, who was both human and divine, as an example for us. In Matthew 25:40, Jesus explains ". . . whatever you did for one of these least brothers of mine, you did for me." God wants us to treat all people, including those who are hungry, thirsty, homeless, or sick, with love and kindness. We know that Jesus, through his life, Death, and Resurrection, is present in everyone.

> **". . . whatever you did for one of these least brothers of mine, you did for me."**
>
> (Matthew 25:40)

 Live It!

What can you do to help care for those whose are homeless, hungry, or elderly? Write one suggestion for each group.

Homeless: _____

Hungry: _____

Elderly: _____

Catholic Morality

Catholic morality is about being respectful, avoiding evil, and doing good. But it is also about much more. It is one of the ways we worship God. In other words, we worship God—align ourselves with God—when we live moral lives. Catholic morality is about growing closer to God and discovering the divine within our neighbors and ourselves. We try to do good and avoid evil. We do this not to get God's approval, but because it helps us align ourselves with God. When we sin, we separate ourselves from God.

Sin and Grace

People don't really like to talk about sin, but we need to understand it because we all sin. To sin is to knowingly offend God or others through our thoughts, words, actions, or when we fail to act appropriately. When we understand sin, we have a greater understanding of our need for God's amazing mercy and grace.

Sin is the ignoring, injuring, or rejecting of our relationship with God. Because God has told us that loving him cannot be separated from love of neighbor, we know that sin is also the ignoring, injuring, or rejecting of our relationship with others. Sin separates us from God and from others.

Grace is our relationship with God. When we are in a state of grace, we are in a healthy relationship with God. We are filled with God's life. For example, when we say "Hail Mary, full of grace," we are saying that Mary is filled with God's life and that she is very close to God.

Grace is not something we can earn. It is a gift from God. God is present for us. We can either accept that relationship or we can ignore it; or worse yet, we can reject it. When we are baptized, we receive the gift of God's grace. We are welcomed into a special relationship with God.

 **Facts of Our Faith:**
Venial and Mortal Sin

The Church teaches that venial sins are those that weaken our relationship with God or with others. Venial sins are less serious than mortal sins, but are still harmful. An example of a venial sin is gossiping about a new student at school. Mortal sins are sins by which we totally break our relationship with God and others and "kill" the life of grace within us. For a sin to be mortal, it must be very serious, the person must know how serious the sin is, and the person freely chooses to do it. An example of a mortal sin is murdering another human being.

Think and Write

Think about how you experience grace in your life. Write a poem that describes what grace means to you.

_____

_____

_____

_____

Capital Sins

The Church gives us a description of seven sinful attitudes, known as Capital Sins. Capital Sins hurt our spiritual health and can lead us to more serious sin. However, we can overcome each of these sins by practicing a virtue, an attitude or way of acting that helps us do good.

- Greed is wanting something so badly that we don't care whom we hurt to get it. When we practice the virtue of generosity, we can avoid greed.
- Envy is wanting someone else's things. We can practice the virtue of kindness to avoid envy.
- Gluttony is eating and drinking way more than we need. We can practice the virtue of temperance to have self-control.
- Lust is doing inappropriate sexual behavior. We can practice chastity, the virtue that helps us respect our bodies and the bodies of others.
- Sloth is not caring to grow spiritually. We can practice the virtue of zeal to help us.
- Anger is wanting to get revenge because we hate someone. We avoid anger by practicing the virtue of gentleness.
- Pride is believing that we are better than others. We can practice the virtue of humility to avoid pride.

Facts of Our Faith: *Sins of Omission*

We can also sin by not doing something. This is known as a sin of omission. In the parable of the rich man and Lazarus in Luke 16:19–21, the rich man doesn't do anything to harm poor Lazarus who sits at his gate. But the fact that the rich man ignores Lazarus makes the rich man guilty of sin. We pray for forgiveness from sins that we commit and sins of omission at Mass in the Penitential Rite. We ask forgiveness for "what I have done and in what I have failed to do."

Think and Write

Think about how we can overcome Capital Sins by practicing virtues. Describe a time when you turned away from a Capital Sin and practiced a virtue instead.

_____

_____

_____

_____

Mercy

Sin is not the end of the story. Like grace, God's mercy is also offered to us as a gift. **Mercy** means compassion and kindness. Mercy is what God always offers us after we sin. God's merciful love calls us out of sin and redeems, or saves us, from every evil and restores our relationship with him. When we respond to God's mercy with repentance and contrition, we are restored to God's grace. Our relationship with God is repaired and made stronger.

Live It!

Sometimes we do things to hurt other people, or sometimes other people hurt us. In either situation, we can try to restore the relationship. Write about a relationship you might need to fix. What can you do to ask for or give forgiveness or mercy?

_____

_____

_____

So What?

So what difference does it make that Catholics believe in human dignity, grace, sin, and mercy? It means that we see living a moral life as an act of worship. It is a way to align ourselves with God, who is love. It means that we cannot separate love of God and love of neighbor. Loving our neighbor is how we encounter God, in whose image we are all made. It means that we try to treat people with respect and care.

Review

Scripture

From within people's hearts can come evil thoughts, unchastity, theft, murder, adultery, greed, malice, deceit, envy, and arrogance. All these evils come from within and they destroy.

(adapted from Mark 7:20–23)

Prayer

Confiteor *(Penitential Act)*

*I confess to almighty God
and to you, my brothers and sisters,
that I have greatly sinned,
in my thoughts and in my words,
in what I have done and in what I have failed to do,
through my fault, through my fault,
through my most grievous fault;
therefore I ask blessed Mary ever-Virgin,
all the Angels and Saints,
and you, my brothers and sisters,
to pray for me to the Lord our God.*

Chapter Highlights

- Love of God and love of neighbor cannot be separated.
- Sin separates us from God.
- Grace and mercy are gifts from God.

Terms to Remember

grace   **mercy**   **moral choice**

React

Why are we called to treat all people with dignity and respect?

_____

_____

At Home

Discuss this question with a grown-up. Write your answer.

What is something you think of as a sin of omission going on in the world around you?

_____

_____

CHAPTER 13

Rules for Living Your Faith

The Commandments, Beatitudes, and Virtues

Does your class have a list of rules to follow?

Which rules are most important? Teachers often have rules to keep order in the classroom. Some rules might be keeping hands and feet to yourself, raising your hand to get out of your seat, and no teasing or bullying. Which rules do you find easy to follow? Which are more difficult? Following the rules, in school and in life, is not always easy. But rules are in place to help and protect us. To align ourselves with God, we need to follow the rules that God gives us. We call these rules the Ten Commandments.

Handbook to Happiness

What are some things that make you happy? Does an A on your report card make you happy? What about getting a new video game? Or talking on the phone with your friends? Or visiting your grandparents?

We all wish to be happy. But what's the "secret" to real happiness, the kind of happiness that is deep inside you? How can we learn the secret?

God does not keep secrets. God has been telling us for thousands of years that there is no secret to finding happiness. The answer is simple: we find happiness in following God's Law of Love. These are known as the Ten Commandments and are sometimes called the Decalogue. God shares the Ten Commandments freely and openly. He gives us the way to happiness. The Ten Commandments are our rules for happiness.

> **The Ten Commandments are our rules for happiness.**

God Shares His Rules for Happiness

God revealed this set of rules to Moses on Mount Sinai in the midst of thunder and lightning. It was not a secret; it was a revelation. God revealed himself to us and his laws through Moses. God wrote his Law of Love on stone tablets and commanded that these be carried in the Ark of the Covenant wherever the people went. This definitely is not how you keep a secret. God wanted to share these rules with us so that we can be happy.

In the Book of Deuteronomy, God talks about his Law of Love and how it is for all of us:

> *"These rules are not mysterious. They are not difficult to understand. They are not out of your reach. No, these rules are already near to you, in your mouths and in your hearts. You need only to follow and obey them."*   (adapted from Deuteronomy 30:11–14)

Jesus continues this revelation in the New Testament, talking about how the kingdom of God is already around us. As you can see, with God, there are no secrets. The code we are to live by is given to us openly and freely.

Think and Write

Choose one rule that is followed in your home. Why is that rule important?

_____

_____

_____

God's Law of Love: The Ten Commandments

A rich young man once approached Jesus and asked, "What must I do to have eternal life?" (adapted from Mark 10:17). Like many people, this young man was searching for more. The man had everything he wanted in life, but still he was missing something. How did Jesus respond? By telling him to live the commandments!

Jesus went on to explain that living the commandments means more than just following a list of rules. It is a way to have a close relationship with God. When we live the commandments, we stay close to God. We don't usually think of rules as a gift, but the Ten Commandments are indeed a gift.

> . . . living the commandments means more than just following a list of rules.

> *Moses gathered the leaders. He told them everything that the LORD had ordered him to tell them. The people responded, "We will do everything that the LORD wants us to do."*
> (adapted from Exodus 19:7–8)

The commandments are the key to maintaining our relationship with God. We follow his Law of Love so that we can continue to enjoy this relationship.

There's a big difference between "not breaking the commandments" and living the commandments. It's not so much that we should worry about breaking a set of rules, but rather how we can use them to build our relationship with God and with others. The Ten Commandments are truly a path for life. Think of them as a map to follow on your way to God. Since the time of Saint Augustine, the Church has required those preparing for Baptism to know the Ten Commandments.

Facts of Our Faith: *Laws Set Us Free*

How exactly do laws set us free? Let's say you want to be free to get an A on a math test. You may feel trapped, however, if you're not sure how to do word problems correctly. If you ask for help from a teacher, tutor, or parent, he or she will help you understand word problems by teaching you the math rules. And if you follow these rules, you will be free to enjoy a good grade on your test. In the same way, following the Ten Commandments helps us avoid any traps we may fall into and frees us to truly love God and others.

The Great Commandment

Someone asked Jesus what the greatest commandment was. "Jesus answered that it is to love the Lord your God with all your heart, soul, mind, and strength, and to love your neighbor as yourself" (adapted from Mark 12:29–31). Does this mean that Jesus changed everything when it comes to the Ten Commandments? No. Jesus was simplifying the Ten Commandments. Jesus helped us to understand the idea that love of God and love of neighbor cannot be separated. To love God, we must love our neighbor. To love God, we must live the commandments.

Is it truly possible to love God above all else and to love our neighbors as ourselves? Yes, because the Ten Commandments are a gift, and God would not give us a gift that we could not use.

The First Commandment: I am the Lord your God. You shall have no other gods before me.

To have no other gods besides the one true God is to put God first in our lives. We put him before popularity (getting invited to a birthday party), accomplishments (winning the baseball trophy), and possessions (your skateboard or favorite stuffed animal).

The Second Commandment: You shall not take the name of the Lord your God in vain.

Names are important. When we first meet someone, we say our name. It's an important step in forming and being part of a friendship. God has given us his name so that we can enter into a relationship with him. The Second Commandment is not just about avoiding swearing, cursing, or using bad language. It's about living in a relationship with God who shares his name so that we get to know him better.

The Third Commandment: Keep holy the Sabbath day.

Did you know that muscles don't actually grow during exercise? Instead, they grow when the body is at rest after exercise. That's when muscles are restored and strengthened. Without rest, our muscles won't grow. In a similar way, without rest, our spiritual muscles won't grow. Resting on the Sabbath day is about caring for the gift of our lives. We rest so that we might be renewed.

The Fourth Commandment: Honor your father and your mother.

We may not like it when someone tells us what to do. We all want to be independent. But we still have to answer to others. Our responsibility to others begins at home, listening to our parents whose responsibility it is to care for us. The Fourth Commandment reminds us that we do not have the last say.

The Fifth Commandment: You shall not kill.

Life is a gift from God. The Fifth Commandment is about being grateful for that gift, from the moment life begins in a mother's body to the moment of death. It reminds us to see God in everyone: in the person who cuts in line in front of us, who treats us unkindly, who dresses differently, or who doesn't look like us. We should appreciate the life of all people, no matter their skin color and traditions.

The Sixth Commandment: You shall not commit adultery.

The Sixth Commandment is about protecting something very good and very precious—our bodies. It is about how we are to share ourselves appropriately and respectfully with others.

The Seventh Commandment: You shall not steal.

The Seventh Commandment is about not taking anything that does not belong to us. This includes obvious items, like money, clothes, toys, and sports equipment. It also refers to the earth and the environment. There are things that have been given for all to share, like the oceans, trees, and animals. Sometimes we forget that we share these things with all of God's creation.

The Eighth Commandment: You shall not bear false witness against your neighbor.

The Eighth Commandment is about more than not telling lies. It is about living so that others can trust us and count on us.

The Ninth Commandment: You shall not covet your neighbor's wife.

We all have wants and desires. The Ninth Commandment reminds us to be sure that our wants and desires keep God first in our lives.

The Tenth Commandment: You shall not covet your neighbor's goods.

Have you ever seen someone break open a piñata? Usually everyone runs to grab as much candy as possible, playfully pushing others out of the way. The Tenth Commandment calls us to be aware of greed and envy, at home and throughout the world. We are brothers and sisters, not competitors.

Live It!

We are called to share the goods of the earth and to protect all of God's creation—people, animals, plants, and the earth. What is one way you can care for each of these groups?

People: _____

Animals: _____

Plants: _____

Earth: _____

The Beatitudes

The **Beatitudes** are the teachings of Jesus in the Sermon on the Mount (Matthew 5:3–10). They invite us to practice loving our neighbors, forgiving others, and helping others. Jesus gives us the Beatitudes, a recipe for happiness, to help us live the Ten Commandments.

Blessed are the poor in spirit, for theirs is the kingdom of heaven. Depend on God first; he will give you all that you need. Money and objects will not bring lasting happiness.

Blessed are they who mourn, for they will be comforted. It's OK to be sad sometimes; it reminds us of how much we need God, who will always heal us.

Blessed are they who hunger and thirst for righteousness, for they will be satisfied. When we believe in honesty, kindness, and doing what is right, God nourishes us and we are at peace.

Blessed are the meek, for they will inherit the land. Be gentle and mild with all of God's creation. God will reward you. Bullying, teasing, and violence never lead to success or happiness.

Blessed are the merciful, for they will be shown mercy. Show love, understanding, and concern for those around you. The more you show, the more you will receive.

Blessed are the clean of heart, for they will see God. Let love be your motivation. When you put God first, he will reveal himself to you.

> **Blessed are the peacemakers, for they will be called children of God.**

Blessed are the peacemakers, for they will be called children of God. Don't build walls and separate yourself from others. Those who make peace are reflecting God's image.

Blessed are they who are persecuted for the sake of righteousness, for theirs is the kingdom of heaven. Stand up for what is right, even though it may be difficult or lonely. When we are treated unkindly for putting God first, his greatness is made known to others.

Blessed are you when they insult you and persecute you and utter every kind of evil against you (falsely) because of me. When we follow the Ten Commandments, our reward is greater and much deeper than an immediate good feeling.

Live It!

Bullying in any form is wrong. What are some reasons a person might be bullied? How can you show that bullying behavior is unacceptable?

_____

_____

_____

The Virtues

What good habits do you have? Do you brush your teeth before you go to bed each night? Do you make your bed every morning? Do you eat fruit every day? Good habits are like muscles; they need to be exercised often if they are to grow strong. The Church teaches seven habits that help us to live as disciples of Jesus. We call these habits **virtues.**

Theological Virtues

The Theological Virtues are faith, hope, and charity.

Faith is the ability to believe in God and give our lives to him. It makes us able to trust God completely and to accept all that God has revealed and taught us.

Hope is the desire for all the good things God has planned for us. Hope gives us confidence that God will always be with us and that we will live with God forever in Heaven.

Charity, sometimes known as love, involves more than just feelings; it is the way we think about God and act toward him and others. "So faith, hope, love remain," Saint Paul writes in 1 Corinthians 13:13, ". . . but the greatest of these is love."

Facts of Our Faith:
Theological Virtues and Cardinal Virtues

Faith, hope, and charity are called Theological Virtues because they come from God and lead to God. Prudence, justice, fortitude, and temperance are called Cardinal Virtues because they are human virtues which we learn through education and doing good things.

Cardinal Virtues

The Cardinal Virtues are prudence, justice, fortitude, and temperance.

Prudence is the ability to decide what is good and then choose to do it. It leads us to stop and think before we act.

Justice is the respect we show for the rights of others and giving them what is rightfully theirs. The just person considers the needs of others and always tries to be fair.

Fortitude is the courage to do what is right, even when it is very difficult. It provides us the strength to resist the temptations we face.

Temperance is the ability to balance what we want with what we need. It helps us build self-control.

Think and Write

Choose two virtues. How can you live each virtue at school?

_____

_____

So What?

So what difference does it make that Catholics believe in the Ten Commandments, the Beatitudes, and the virtues? God openly tells us, through the Ten Commandments and through Jesus Christ, how we are to live. The Beatitudes and the virtues help us to live out the commandments. God's Law of Love, the Ten Commandments, is a gift that helps us to live a life that is blessed with God's presence.

Review

Scripture

The Pharisees asked, "When will the kingdom of God come?" Jesus replied, "The kingdom of God cannot be seen. And no one will point to it and announce that it is here. That is because it is already around you."   (adapted from Luke 17:20–21)

Prayer

Thank you, God, for the gift of the Ten Commandments. Thank you for showing us how we are to live for us to remain in close relationship with you. Amen.

Chapter Highlights

- God openly and freely reveals the way to happiness.
- The Ten Commandments are God's Law of Love.
- The Beatitudes help us live according to God's Law of Love.
- The virtues are seven habits that help us live as disciples of Jesus.

Terms to Remember

Beatitudes   **virtue**

React

Two ways I live out the commandments at home:

_____

_____

Two ways I live out the commandments at school:

_____

_____

At Home

Discuss these questions with a grown-up. Write your answers.

Which of the commandments do you think our society needs to follow most? Why?

_____

_____

CHAPTER 14

Works of Mercy and Social Justice

 **Imagine you are playing kickball when your best friend falls and twists his ankle.** Your friend can't walk, and you can see his ankle swelling up, but most of the kids want to continue playing the game. What would you do? You would most likely find a grown-up to help your friend. Helping our friends when they are hurt is something we do out of love. God expects us to take this a step further. He wants us to help all people who are in need. The Catholic Church gives us the Corporal Works of Mercy and the Spiritual Works of Mercy to show us how to help share God's love with others.

The Corporal Works of Mercy

If you had a sandwich for lunch and your best friend forgot her lunch, would you eat your sandwich without offering her half of it? Probably not. By sharing your sandwich with your friend, you are showing mercy. Mercy is showing others kindness, compassion, and forgiveness.

We do not perform good works to make God happy. We do good works because we want to be close to God. By sharing with others, we see the living God. The Catholic Church identifies for us different works of mercy—The Corporal Works of Mercy and the Spiritual Works of Mercy—to show us how to live for others.

The **Corporal Works of Mercy** are ways we can help our neighbors with everyday physical needs. Here are some ways we can practice these works.

Feed the hungry Bring canned goods to food pantries, soup kitchens, and other organizations that feed those who are hungry. Volunteer alongside your parents.

Give drink to the thirsty Be mindful of ways that ensure everyone will have clean water to drink. Use environmentally friendly laundry detergents and conserve water while brushing your teeth or doing the dishes.

Clothe the naked Go through your drawers and closets to find clothes in good condition to donate to the Society of St. Vincent de Paul or other organizations that accept clothing; donate baby clothes for babies in need; participate in clothing drives at your school or in your community.

Shelter the homeless Help neighbors to care for their homes and do repairs; donate to or volunteer for Catholic Charities, the Catholic Campaign for Human Development, and Habitat for Humanity.

Visit the sick Spend time with those who are sick or can't leave their homes; take the time to call, send a card, or e-mail someone who is sick.

Visit the imprisoned Pray for or visit people "imprisoned" by loneliness, sickness, or old age.

Bury the dead Attend wakes and funerals; provide food baskets to care centers; go with relatives to the cemetery; send sympathy cards.

Facts of Our Faith:
*The Society of
St. Vincent de Paul*

The Society of St. Vincent de Paul is one of many Catholic organizations that addresses the Corporal Works of Mercy. The society provides medical supplies, food for those in need, counseling and education programs, and other services. The society was started in Paris in 1833 and began in the United States in St. Louis, Missouri, in 1845. With an adult, learn more about the society by checking out their web site or through your local diocese.

Think and Write

Read this verse adapted from James 2:18: "Someone might say: 'You have faith and I have works. Show your faith to me without works, and I will show my faith to you from my works.'" Write what you think the verse means.

_____

_____

Live It!

Choose one of the Corporal Acts of Mercy. Write an action plan for ways to practice that act of mercy during the next month.

_____

_____

_____

_____

The Spiritual Works of Mercy

The Church also identifies works of mercy to provide for spiritual and emotional needs. These are called the **Spiritual Works of Mercy.** Here are ways we can practice them.

Counsel the doubtful Be positive; offer to pray for people who are sad or struggling; encourage people to put their hope and trust in God.

Instruct the ignorant Learn about the Catholic faith and share what you know with others; tutor classmates who struggle; teach younger siblings prayers and read books to them.

Admonish sinners Stand up for things you believe in like treating others with respect; if children tease or bully, ask them to stop or get an adult to help; do not gossip; set a good example.

Comfort the afflicted Walk with others through their pain; offer words of encouragement to those who seem discouraged; offer sympathy to those who are grieving.

Forgive offenses Pray for those who have hurt you and pray for the courage to forgive; ask forgiveness from others; let go of grudges; go out of your way to be positive with those whom you are having a difficult time.

Bear wrongs patiently Try not to be critical of others; overlook others' mistakes; give people the benefit of the doubt; pray for those who have hurt you.

Pray for the living and the dead Say prayers for loved ones who have died; make a list of people who you know are sick and pray for them every day.

The key to all the works of mercy is that they do not happen by accident. For them to happen, we must decide to practice them. The Works of Mercy can change society. When we share merciful love with others, we share in God's work of transforming the world.

 Think and Write

Write about a situation in which you might practice one of the Spiritual Works of Mercy.

_____

_____

_____

Catholic Social Teaching

What is social justice? **Social justice** is about making sure that society helps all people to live with dignity and respect. The key to social justice is the common good. The common good is the well-being of the whole community. The Catholic Church has a long tradition of making society better by living out the Gospel message. We call this tradition Catholic Social Teaching. These are the principles of Catholic Social Teaching.

Life and Dignity of the Human Person All human life is sacred. We are called to respect and value people over things and to ask whether what we do respects or harms the dignity of people.

Call to Family, Community, and Participation Our faith and society need healthy families and healthy communities. We must support and strengthen families.

Rights and Responsibilities Every person has a right to life and a right for human decency. When we protect these basic human rights, we build a healthy society.

Option for the Poor and Vulnerable In our world, many people are very rich while others are very poor. We are called to try to meet the material needs of those who are poor.

The Dignity of Work and the Rights of Workers Workers have basic rights that must be respected. These include the right to work, to fair wages, to private property, to organize and join unions, and to look for economic opportunity.

Solidarity Because God is our Father, we are all brothers and sisters, with the responsibility to care for one another. Solidarity is the attitude to share with one another our spiritual and material goods and to know that we can count on one another.

Care for God's Creation God is the Creator of all people and all things, and he wants us to enjoy his creation. We are called to make good choices that protect all of God's creation.

When we work to apply these principles, we are living the Gospel message.

 ## Live It!

Design a bumper sticker that goes along with one of the principles of Catholic Social Teaching. Use the examples to help you.

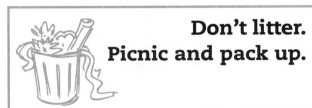

A Powerful Pair: Mercy and Justice

Mercy and **justice** go hand in hand. Both help us show love for others, but justice takes mercy a step further. For example, when we feed those who are hungry, we are performing a work of mercy. But when we work to find a way to get rid of causes of hunger, we are working for justice. When we donate bottled water to a community with a polluted water supply, we are doing a work of mercy. When we write letters to senators and members of Congress to encourage them to clean up the water supply, we are working for justice.

 Think and Write

For each need, write a way to show mercy and a way to work for justice.

Need	Mercy	Justice
Homelessness		
Hunger		
Poverty		
Water Pollution		

Facts of Our Faith: *A Tireless Worker for Justice and Mercy*

Dorothy Day cofounded the Catholic Worker Movement in 1933. Dorothy Day is an example of a person who worked for both mercy and justice. She opened houses for homeless people, and she took part in demonstrations for workers' rights. She is an amazing example of the Gospel in action.

Live It!

Write acts of mercy and ways to work for justice on strips of paper. Place them in a Mercy mug and a Justice jar. As you continue your journey of faith, choose a slip of paper from one jar each week. During the following week, find a way to act on the need you chose.

So What?

So what difference does it make that Catholics believe in works of mercy and social justice? It means that we feel solidarity with all people, and that by showing mercy to others, we share in God's love of the world.

Review

Scripture

But a Samaritan traveler who came upon him was moved with compassion at the sight. He approached the victim, poured oil and wine over his wounds and bandaged them. Then he lifted him up on his own animal, took him to an inn and cared for him. The next day he took out two silver coins and gave them to the innkeeper with the instruction, "Take care of him. If you spend more than what I have given you, I shall repay you on my way back." Which of these three, in your opinion, was neighbor to the robbers' victim? He answered, "The one who treated him with mercy." Jesus said to him, "Go and do likewise."   (Luke 10:33–37)

Prayer

Holy Trinity, help me to unselfishly share with others and help with their physical and spiritual needs. Amen.

Chapter Highlights

- The Corporal Works of Mercy address the physical needs of people.
- The Spiritual Works of Mercy address the emotional and spiritual needs of people.
- When we perform acts of mercy, we are living out the Gospel message.
- Catholic Social Teaching principles are based on working for justice for all people.

Terms to Remember

Corporal Works of Mercy	**social justice**
justice	**Spiritual Works of Mercy**

React

Two ways I can promote social justice in my community:

_____

_____

At Home

Discuss this question with a grown-up. Write your answer.

What is one principle of Catholic Social Teaching you see being practiced in your community?

_____

CHAPTER 15

Conscience and Decision Making

 **Imagine you have a big science test in class tomorrow.** You have studied hard and feel prepared to take it. You know your friend Matt has not studied at all for the test. He has been working all week on a history project and forgot to study for the science test. When you get to school in the morning, Matt asks if you will let him see your test as you take it so that he can copy the answers. What do you think about what Matt is asking you to do? How can you make the right choice? What is that little voice in your head telling you to do?

Look Before You Leap

When you have a difficult choice to make, how do you decide what to do? The thinking, or voice inside your head, that helps you decide is your **conscience.** Your conscience is what guides you to do the right thing in most situations. Conscience is a gift that can guide us through life. Our conscience must be formed so that we make choices that keep us close to God. We begin to learn right from wrong from our parents, family members, and teachers. We continue to develop a good conscience through our whole lives. A well-formed conscience can help us choose before we act. Our conscience also helps us look at our choices and decide if they were good or bad after we act.

Forming Your Conscience

So how do you work on forming a good conscience—one that understands the difference between right and wrong? The Church understands that we must always listen to our own consciences. Here are some basic ways to form a conscience:

- Learn from our mistakes and those of others.
- Pray to the Holy Spirit for guidance.
- Read and listen to Scripture.
- Learn and take to heart the teachings of the Church.
- Think about what our decisions might do to other people.

 Think and Write

You and your brother were throwing a ball around the living room. Your dad always asks you not to throw a ball in the house. You throw the ball and it hits a picture frame. The frame falls and breaks. Write about what you would do in this situation.

_____

_____

_____

 Live It!

Imagine you have a friend who sometimes asks you to do things that are wrong. What can you say so that she understands why you want to make good choices?

_____

_____

Put On Your Thinking Cap

Have your parents ever asked "What were you thinking?" Parents usually ask this after they have found their children making a poor decision. They ask the question even though they know the child probably didn't give his or her decision much thought at all.

Good, moral decision making requires us to think before we act. We are called to love the Lord God with our entire heart, soul, mind, and strength. This means that the choices and decisions we make in life require thinking before we act.

What kind of thinking goes into making a good moral choice? Although the choices themselves are not easy, the steps we can use are. Here are three questions you can ask yourself when you have a decision to make:

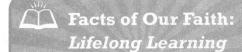

Facts of Our Faith:
Lifelong Learning

Because we know that following Jesus requires faith and thinking, we try to continue learning about our faith and forming our conscience throughout our entire lives. Many people think that Confirmation represents our graduation from religious education. Not so! The process of conscience formation begins when we are very young, but we need to continue this process throughout our lives.

- Is the thing I'm choosing to do a good thing? For example, Claire finds a hat on the playground. She thinks the hat is really nice, but decides to bring it to the Lost and Found box.
- Am I choosing to do it for the right reasons? Claire knows that the hat is not hers. The owner will be looking for it.
- Am I choosing to do it at the right time and place? Claire brings the hat to the Lost and Found box right away to help a person find her hat as soon as possible.

Think and Write

Think of a time when you had to make a difficult decision. Explain how you would use the three questions above if you had to make the decision again. Tell if your decision would be the same or different and why.

_____

_____

_____

_____

What Would Jesus Do?

Jesus came to earth and became man. As a man, he was often faced with difficult decisions, just like all of us. What did Jesus do when he had to make a difficult choice? This story from the Gospel of Matthew can help us understand.

> **What did Jesus do when he had to make a difficult choice?**

The Holy Spirit led Jesus into the desert for 40 days and 40 nights. Jesus was fasting—he did not eat for the whole time. The Devil tempted him three times. The first time he asked him to turn stones into bread. Jesus said, "The Scriptures say that people do not live only on bread, but on every word that God speaks."

The next time the Devil took Jesus to the top of the Temple. He said, "If you are the Son of God, throw yourself down. The Scriptures say that God will tell the angels to protect you." Jesus answered, "The Scriptures also say you should not put God to the test."

The last time, the Devil took Jesus to a high mountain and showed him all the kingdoms of the world. He said, "All these I shall give you if you worship me." Jesus replied, "Go away, Satan! The Scriptures say you shall worship God alone and serve only him."

Then the Devil left Jesus and the angels came and cared for him.

(adapted from Matthew 4:1–11)

Jesus faced three difficult choices from the Devil. But he thought about what Scripture said and knew what God would want him to do. We can pray to the Holy Spirit for help, read Scripture, ask people we trust for advice, and learn what the Church teaches. All of these things can help us make good moral choices.

 Facts of Our Faith: *Scripture and Decision Making*

There are many stories in the Bible that teach us how to make good decisions. Jesus used parables to teach us right from wrong and to help people understand how God wants us to act. Jesus taught the Golden Rule in Matthew 7:12, "Do to others whatever you would have them do to you." Reading Scripture stories and verses is one thing we can use to help us make good decisions.

Live It!

Imagine that you and your parents are walking to your car in a parking lot near a fast-food restaurant and a young woman with a small child asks you for money. She says that her child is hungry and that they have no money. What might be a good moral choice?

_____

_____

_____

_____

So What?

So what difference does it make that Catholics believe in having a fully formed conscience and in making good moral decisions? It means that we are called to be thinkers. It means that we must continue to learn about our Catholic faith our whole lives so that we can learn to see things as God sees them. To follow Jesus, we must be aware of what he teaches us and use it to make good choices.

Review

Scripture

The aim of this instruction is love from a pure heart, a good conscience, and a sincere faith. Some people have turned away from these and turned to meaningless talk, and they do not understand what they are saying. . . . I know you will have faith and a good conscience. Some, by not listening to their conscience, have made a shipwreck of their faith.

(adapted from 1 Timothy 1:5–7, 18–19)

Prayer

Loving God, send your Holy Spirit to open my mind so that I might follow you more closely. Help me to form my conscience so that I can come to see myself, others, and the world as you see them. Help me to think so that I might act according to your will. Amen.

Chapter Highlights

- Our conscience guides us to do the right thing.
- We must form a good conscience throughout our lives.
- Catholic teachings encourage us to think before we act.

Term to Remember

conscience

React

Two things I can do to help form a good conscience:

_____

_____

Three questions I can ask myself about difficult decisions:

_____

_____

_____

At Home

Discuss this question with a grown-up. Write your answer.

What is one choice that people can make today to help people and all of God's creation?

_____

_____

PART 4

Prayer: Praying Faith

"Ask and it will be given to you; seek and you will find; knock and the door will be opened to you. For everyone who asks, receives; and the one who seeks, finds; and to the one who knocks, the door will be opened. Which one of you would hand his son a stone when he asks for a loaf of bread, or a snake when he asks for a fish? If you then, who are wicked, know how to give good gifts to your children, how much more will your heavenly Father give good things to those who ask him."

Matthew 7:7–11

CHAPTER 16

Prayer

 When you hear a phone ringing, what do you want to do? Of course, you want to pick it up and find out who is calling. Today, with caller ID and cell phones, we don't even have to answer to know who's calling. But we still want to answer the phone. We want to know why people are calling and to find out what's going on in their lives. God is always calling us. He doesn't just call on us every now and then. It's like he is always calling us, waiting for us to get back to him. The way to answer God's call is through prayer. Prayer keeps us connected with God.

God Is Calling

Imagine this. The phone rings, Eduardo answers it, and the conversation begins.

Eduardo says, "Hello!"

The person on the other end responds, "Well, hello Eduardo, how are you? I haven't heard from you in a while."

"Who is this?" asks Eduardo.

"Eduardo, this is God. You haven't called lately. I'm waiting to hear from you. I'm sure there are things we can talk about," says God.

> **All prayer is a response to God.**

What do you think Eduardo is thinking? Of course, it's a little silly to think that God would call someone on the phone, but use your imagination. Eduardo is probably thinking "Oh my, when was the last time I prayed? I guess I really have been out of touch with God. I had forgotten all about him." How do you think he feels about this phone call? How would you feel if you got a similar call from God?

The idea of God calling us is really not that silly. This is a way we can think about God. God's line is always open for us. He is waiting patiently to hear our prayers and give us help and guidance. We just have to learn to make prayer a part of our lives.

God is always trying to get our attention. In Chapter 2, we learned that God takes the initiative. God calls, and we are invited to respond. All prayer is a response to God. He is actively inviting us to recognize his loving presence. Prayer shows that we are noticing his presence in our lives. **Prayer** is our response to his constant invitation.

Keeping the Conversation Going

Saint Paul said, "Pray without ceasing" (1 Thessalonians 5:17). Of course, this doesn't mean that we are constantly talking to God. Prayer describes all the ways we recognize and respond to God's presence. Prayer might be listening to a friend who is upset, recognizing God's care for him. We can recognize God in a beautiful sunny day after a week of rain. We can recognize God in the midst of the rain. When we see or do these things and know that God is part of them, we are praying.

There are many times we can include prayer in our lives. We can start the day with prayer. We can pray before meals. We can offer prayers when we see or hear about someone who is sick. We can thank God for good things that happen throughout the day. We can say bedtime prayers. When we pray, we can pray prayers we know or just talk with God. We can also sit quietly and listen. All of these things help us be in touch with God.

> Prayer is our response to God's constant effort to reach our hearts.

To pray "without ceasing" means living our lives in constant communion with God. It means being aware of God's presence all around us. Sometimes we will use words to communicate. Most of the time we silently recognize God's presence. Prayer is our response to God's constant effort to reach our hearts.

 Think and Write

Write a prayer of adoration, petition, intercession, thanksgiving, or praise.

_____

_____

_____

_____

_____

_____

_____

 Facts of Our Faith:
Basic Ways of Praying

Our communication with God can be done in different ways. The Church identifies the following forms of prayer:

- **Adoration** Recognizing God's greatness
- **Petition** Asking God to take care of our personal needs
- **Intercession** Praying for the needs of others
- **Thanksgiving** Thanking God for all his good gifts
- **Praise** Joyfully saying that God is God

Lift Up Your Hearts

The *Catechism of the Catholic Church* describes prayer as "the raising of one's mind and heart to God" (2559). At Mass, the priest invites us to "lift up your hearts." We respond "We lift them up to the Lord." Just what does it mean to "raise" or "lift up" our hearts? When we lift up our hearts, we realize God is at the center of our lives. We lift up our hearts to God in Heaven. To lift up our hearts means to be joined with God.

Sometimes people talk about the power of prayer. What they are saying is that when we join with God, we open ourselves up to the divine life within us. God's divine life changes us. Through prayer, we can live lives filled with faith, hope, and love.

! **Live It!**

Write about two new times you could include prayer during this week.

_____

_____

_____

Pray for Victory?

Imagine that two rival soccer teams in your town are playing one another in the championship game. Parents, friends, and team members gather before the game. They are trying to build team spirit. Someone suggests that everyone pray for a victory. Is this a good idea? Should they pray to win the championship?

These kinds of stories can sometimes confuse us. The purpose of prayer is not to influence God. Prayer does not change God. Prayer changes us. The other team might have also been praying for a win. Do we really think that God decides which team to lead to victory based on the quality of prayers? Of course not. But that brings up a question, "So then, why pray at all?"

For example, should we pray for

- no rain during a parade?
- help in winning a drawing contest?
- help in passing a math test?
- peace in the world?

Of course, the answer is "Yes, yes, YES!" But we must know what we are praying for and why we pray. We pray for one reason only: to align ourselves with God's will. God's will is what God wants for us. In each of these situations, we are praying about something very important to us, trying to align our will with God's will. No matter how the situation turns out, God steps in because God is always stepping in.

Unfortunately only when we get what we want and think it's a miracle do we think that God was involved. Miracles do happen, but Jesus pointed out that the greatest miracle is the transformation of a human heart. When Jesus was asked to heal a man who was paralyzed, he told him that his sins were forgiven. When the Pharisees protested that only God can forgive sins, Jesus asked, "Which is easier to say, 'Your sins are forgiven,' or to say 'Rise and walk'?" (Matthew 9:5). Jesus was pointing out that the forgiveness of sin—the transformation of this man's heart—was a greater miracle than the healing of this man's paralysis. The physical healing, which was the visible miracle, was an outward sign of the greater invisible miracle—the healing of the human heart.

> **We pray for one reason only: to align ourselves with God's will.**

And so, we pray

- for no rain during a parade; and if it does rain, we continue to pray so that we can learn what God's will is for us for the day.
- for us to win the drawing contest; knowing that what we are really praying for is that we will do our best and that the winner will be the person who draws better on that day. And if we do not win, we continue to pray to help us accept the loss, to learn from it, to grow from it, and to move on with the right attitude.
- for help on an exam; not to avoid studying, but to use the gift of our minds.
- for world peace; because we know that it is God's will and that any lack of peace is the result of people not able to work things out among themselves.

Think and Write

Think about what you have read about prayer. Describe prayer in your own words.

_____

_____

_____

_____

_____

_____

So Why Does God Allow Evil to Happen?

God does not cause bad things to happen. When someone gets seriously ill or dies, that is part of being human. These things do not happen because that person was sinful. Some pain and suffering is brought about by human sinfulness, when people hurt other people. God does not will for that suffering to happen, but has given people the free will to choose between good and evil. If we choose evil, other people will be hurt in the process. Also, God does not will natural disasters like hurricanes and tornadoes to hurt and kill people. When God created the earth, that included the natural science of weather. Weather can be both pleasant or frightening for people.

Where is God when suffering is happening? He is with us, just as he was with Jesus when he was on the cross. God's presence in times of suffering helps us to see beyond the pain that we do not understand. He helps us to see that we are always close to him and will someday see Salvation. This is why Catholics display crucifixes. We recognize that we will be saved from all suffering and given new life, just as Jesus was given new life after his suffering on the cross.

Facts of Our Faith:
The Book of Job

The Book of Job tells the story of Job, a man who faces difficult situations. In the end, however, the Book of Job tells us that suffering is part of the mystery of life and that we cannot hope to fully understand it. The Book of Job inspires us to bow our heads when we are suffering and to turn to God, who alone can comfort us.

Live It!

Write a prayer for peace in your community and in the world. Pray the prayer each day this week.

_____

_____

_____

So What?

So what difference does it make that Catholics believe in prayer? It means that we are confident that we are not alone—God is with us. It means that we know that we don't have to get God's attention. We know that God is always seeking our attention and inviting us to be close to him. It means that we are in a loving relationship with God and through this relationship that we can grow in holiness. It means that God gives us the help we need to lift up our hearts and center our lives on him.

Review

Scripture

I raise my eyes toward the mountains. / From whence shall come my help? / My help comes from the LORD, / the maker of heaven and earth. / He will not allow your foot to slip; / or your guardian to sleep. / Behold, the guardian of Israel / never slumbers nor sleeps. (Psalm 121:1–4)

Prayer

Loving God, thank you for inviting me to be close to you. Help me to recognize this invitation and to respond with thankfulness every day. Holy Spirit, teach me to pray so that I may grow closer to the Father through Jesus. Help me to not only talk to God but also to listen to the ways that God is speaking to me. Amen.

Chapter Highlights

- Prayer is our response to God's invitation to us.
- To pray without ceasing means to live our lives in constant communion with God.
- We have many forms of prayer available to us to help us keep in touch with our loving God.

Term to Remember

prayer

React

Write three different ways to communicate with God through prayer.

_____

_____

_____

At Home

Discuss this question with a grown-up. Write your answer.

What is one thing happening in your community that people can pray for?

_____

_____

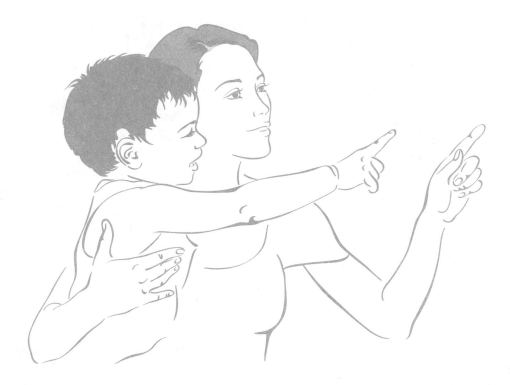

CHAPTER 17

Forms of Prayer

 **Think about how babies let their parents know what they need without being able to speak.**

They cry, they make noises, they smile, and they laugh. Think about how pets communicate with us. Dogs bark, growl, and nudge you with their heads. Cats purr. What are some ways people communicate without talking? People smile, frown, laugh, and cry. We use hand gestures, shake hands, hold hands, clap, and point. We also can communicate with God without using words.

Different Ways of Communicating

Think about the people you are closest to such as your parents, your brothers or sisters, and your best friends. How do you communicate with them? Mostly you use words. But sometimes you can just look at them and know exactly what they are thinking. Sometimes it just takes a smile or a pat on the back to get a message across. Is one form of communication better than another? No. They are just different.

Prayer works the same way. There is vocal prayer, which is praying using words. There is also contemplative prayer, which is prayer that moves into silence. These are just different ways we communicate with God.

When we start to make prayer a part of our lives, we mostly use words to talk to God. As we grow older, we may find ourselves relying less on words and more on listening to God. These are just different ways of being in communion with God. And don't forget that God also speaks to us in many different ways.

> ### Facts of Our Faith:
> ### *The* Catechism *and Prayer*
>
> Prayer is so important to our faith that in the *Catechism of the Catholic Church,* there is an entire section about prayer. "Where does prayer come from? . . . According to Scripture, it is the *heart* that prays." (*CCC* 2562) Do you pray from your heart?

Vocal Prayer

Vocal prayer is prayer with words either spoken aloud or in the silence of our hearts. This is the most natural form of prayer. For most people, it is the place where prayer begins.

Traditional Prayers

Traditional prayers are like family treasures that have been handed down to us by the Church. Traditional prayers are helpful for the times when we cannot find the words of our own to pray. They also help groups of people to pray together. Some of the best-known examples include the following:

- Sign of the Cross
- Lord's Prayer (Our Father)
- Hail Mary
- Glory Be to the Father (Doxology)
- Prayer Before Meals
- Prayer After Meals
- Act of Contrition
- Hail, Holy Queen (*Salve Regina*)
- Prayer to the Holy Spirit
- Apostles' Creed

Spontaneous Prayer

Because Catholics have so many traditional prayers, we are sometimes not familiar with spontaneous prayer. Spontaneous prayer is prayer using our own words. God answers to many names. For example, you may begin by saying Dear God, Heavenly Father, Almighty God, Dear Jesus, Creator of All Things, or Loving God.

When you talk to God, you can use these four steps to help you remember how to practice spontaneous prayer. A fun way to remember these steps is G-I-F-T.

1. **G**ive thanks. Being thankful reminds us that God takes the first step and we are now responding. Offer thanks for simple things like being able to ride your bike outside or reading a book to your little cousin.
2. **I**dentify your needs. Tell God what you are worried about. Ask for help dealing with something that is worrying you.
3. **F**orgive and be forgiven. Ask for forgiveness for anything you may have done wrong. Pray for the grace to forgive others.
4. **T**hink of others. We never just pray for ourselves. We think of what other people may need.

Think and Write

Use the steps described above to write your own spontaneous prayer.

_____

_____

_____

Meditation

Meditation, or reflective prayer, is thinking about God. Sometimes people use Scripture passages, inspirational readings, or sacred images to help them meditate. When we meditate, we try to think about God's presence in our lives. There are five common prayers Catholics use for meditation. They are the Rosary, the Stations of the Cross, the Daily Examen, reflective prayer, and the *lectio divina* (LECT-see-oh dih-VEE-nah).

The Rosary

When you pray the Rosary, you use vocal, meditative, and contemplative forms of prayer. During the Rosary, we meditate on the events of the lives of Jesus and his mother, Mary, while we pray the words of the Lord's Prayer, the Hail Mary, and the Glory Be to the Father. Each event is called a mystery. The four mysteries are explained on page 136.

A rosary is made up of a string of beads and a crucifix. We begin praying the Rosary by holding the crucifix in our hands as we pray the Sign of the Cross. Then we pray the Apostles' Creed.

Next to the crucifix, there is a single bead followed by a set of three beads and another single bead. We Pray the Lord's Prayer as we hold the first single bead and a Hail Mary at each bead in the set of three that follows. Then we pray the Glory Be to the Father. On the next single bead, we think about the first mystery and pray the Lord's Prayer.

There are five sets of ten beads; each set is called a decade. We pray a Hail Mary on each bead of a decade as we reflect on a particular mystery in the lives of Jesus and Mary. We pray the Glory Be to the Father at the end of each decade. Many people pray the Hail, Holy Queen after the last decade. Between decades is a single bead on which we think about one of the mysteries and pray the Lord's Prayer.

We end by holding the crucifix as we pray the Sign of the Cross.

Facts of Our Faith:
Praying in Communion with Mary

For Catholics, the Blessed Virgin Mary connects us to her Son, Jesus, in a special way. Because she is the mother of Jesus, we can go to her for help in growing closer to him. We do not pray to Mary, but we pray in communion with her, knowing that through her we can come to know her Son, Jesus.

Praying the Rosary

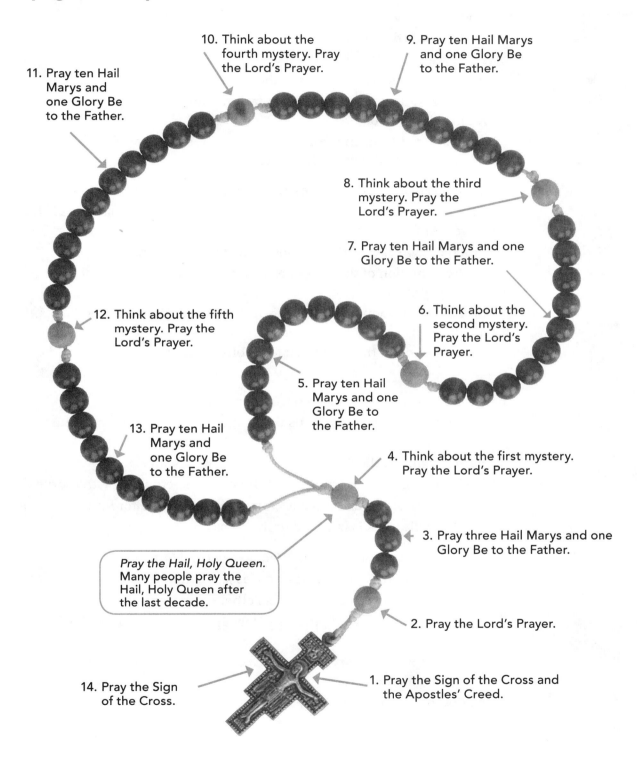

11. Pray ten Hail Marys and one Glory Be to the Father.

10. Think about the fourth mystery. Pray the Lord's Prayer.

9. Pray ten Hail Marys and one Glory Be to the Father.

8. Think about the third mystery. Pray the Lord's Prayer.

7. Pray ten Hail Marys and one Glory Be to the Father.

12. Think about the fifth mystery. Pray the Lord's Prayer.

6. Think about the second mystery. Pray the Lord's Prayer.

5. Pray ten Hail Marys and one Glory Be to the Father.

13. Pray ten Hail Marys and one Glory Be to the Father.

4. Think about the first mystery. Pray the Lord's Prayer.

3. Pray three Hail Marys and one Glory Be to the Father.

Pray the Hail, Holy Queen. Many people pray the Hail, Holy Queen after the last decade.

2. Pray the Lord's Prayer.

14. Pray the Sign of the Cross.

1. Pray the Sign of the Cross and the Apostles' Creed.

The Mysteries of the Rosary

The Joyful Mysteries (prayed on Mondays and Saturdays)

The Annunciation: Mary learns that she will be the mother of Jesus.

The Visitation: Mary visits Elizabeth.

The Nativity: Jesus is born in a stable in Bethlehem.

The Presentation: Mary and Joseph take the infant Jesus to the Temple to present him to God.

The Finding of Jesus in the Temple: Jesus is found in the Temple, discussing his faith with the teachers.

The Luminous Mysteries or The Mysteries of Light (prayed on Thursdays)

The Baptism of Jesus in the River Jordan: God proclaims that Jesus is his beloved Son.

The Wedding Feast at Cana: Jesus performs his first miracle.

The Proclamation of the Kingdom of God: Jesus calls all to conversion and service to the kingdom.

The Transfiguration of Jesus: Jesus is revealed in glory to Peter, James, and John.

The Institution of the Eucharist: Jesus offers his Body and Blood at the Last Supper.

The Sorrowful Mysteries (prayed on Tuesdays and Fridays)

The Agony in the Garden: Jesus prays in the Garden of Gethsemane on the night before he dies.

The Scourging at the Pillar: Jesus is beaten with whips.

The Crowning with Thorns: Jesus is mocked and crowned with thorns.

The Carrying of the Cross: Jesus carries the cross used for his Crucifixion.

The Crucifixion: Jesus is nailed to the cross and dies.

The Glorious Mysteries (prayed on Wednesdays and Sundays)

The Resurrection: God the Father raises Jesus from the dead.

The Ascension: Jesus returns to his Father in Heaven.

The Coming of the Holy Spirit: The Holy Spirit comes to bring new life to the disciples.

The Assumption of Mary: At the end of her life on earth, Mary is taken body and soul into Heaven.

The Coronation of Mary: Mary is crowned as Queen of Heaven and Earth.

Live It!

Write a prayer intention for a problem that has been in the news this week. As a class, pray a Rosary for all your intentions.

_____

_____

_____

Stations of the Cross

The **Stations of the Cross** represent events from Jesus' Passion, Death, and Resurrection. At each station, we pause and use our senses and imagination to meditate on the scene pictured or described. We can pray in our own words, or we can use prayers provided in a Stations of the Cross prayer book. Below is a description of each station.

1. Jesus is condemned to death.
2. Jesus takes up his cross.
3. Jesus falls the first time.
4. Jesus meets his sorrowful mother.
5. Simon of Cyrene helps Jesus carry the cross.
6. Veronica wipes the face of Jesus.
7. Jesus falls a second time.
8. Jesus meets the women of Jerusalem.
9. Jesus falls the third time.
10. Jesus is stripped of his garments.
11. Jesus is nailed to the cross.
12. Jesus dies on the cross.
13. Jesus is taken down from the cross.
14. Jesus is laid in the tomb.

The closing prayer, which is sometimes included as a 15th station, reflects on the Resurrection of Jesus.

Daily Examen

Saint Ignatius of Loyola developed a simple method of meditation called the Daily Examen. We can use this meditation at the end of the day to think back about how the day was and to recognize how God is active in our daily lives. We can follow these steps:

- Set aside 10–15 minutes near the end of the day.
- Quiet yourself and think about God's presence, thanking God for his love and asking the Holy Spirit for guidance.
- Review your day, thanking God for the ways he blessed you.

- Review your day again, thinking about the opportunities you had to use the gifts God has given you. When did you use God's gifts? When could you have used them but didn't?
- Thank God for the ways you grew closer to him, and ask forgiveness for the opportunities you missed or decided against.
- Decide to be closer to God's grace in the days to come and end the meditation with the Lord's Prayer.

Reflective Prayer

Also known as meditation, reflective prayer helps us use our minds and imagination to have a prayerful conversation with God. It also helps us recognize his presence in our daily lives. Follow these steps:

- Set aside 10–15 minutes and find a quiet place where you can be comfortable. Close your eyes, or focus on a religious picture or a lighted candle. You can also listen to quiet instrumental music in the background.
- Relax yourself by slowly and silently taking a deep breath and then let it out slowly. You can establish a rhythm by slowly counting to three while breathing in and slowly counting to three while breathing out. If you concentrate on your breaths, it will help quiet your thoughts.
- Prayerfully read a brief passage from the Gospels and imagine yourself in the story. Use your imagination to talk with Jesus and listen to him speak to you. Instead of Scripture, you can use prayer books or sacred objects, such as a crucifix or an icon, a religious image, to help you focus on God. Talk to Jesus as you would talk to a friend.
- End your reflection with one or two minutes of contemplation—simply resting quietly in the hands of God.

Lectio Divina

For many centuries, Catholics have used a form of meditation called *lectio divina*. In Latin, it means "sacred reading." This is a way of spending time with the Word of God, using a special form of reading and listening. It's like the Rosary in that you use vocal, meditative, and contemplative forms of prayer. First, you read a brief Scripture passage, then you reflect. Next, you pray in silent conversation with God and end your meditation by resting in God's presence.

Contemplative Prayer

While meditation involves actively focusing, contemplation is simply resting quietly in God's presence. In contemplation, we do not try to speak to God, but take in God's glory and love all around us. No words are needed.

Centering Prayer

Centering prayer is a kind of contemplative prayer. Centering prayer invites us to open our minds and hearts to God's presence in silence. It allows us to receive God's gift of grace. Following these steps will help:

- Choose a "sacred word" or phrase such as "Come, Lord Jesus," "Peace," or "Abba."
- Find a comfortable position and close your eyes. Sit silently for a few moments.
- Think about your sacred words to help you receive God's grace. In your mind, repeat this word or phrase occasionally, especially when you begin to think of other things.
- When you are ready, set aside your sacred words and just rest in silence.
- Try to give yourself 20 minutes for centering prayer.

We begin to see the effect of centering prayer, like most prayer, over time. It helps us lift our minds and hearts to God. It helps us see God's presence in our lives.

Think and Write

Choose one method of prayer that is new to you. Take 10 minutes to pray using the new form of prayer. In a few words, describe your experience.

_____

_____

Live It!

Add a new prayer form into your family prayer time. Describe how you can do this.

_____

_____

So What?

What difference does it make that Catholics have so many forms of prayer? It means that, no matter our personality type, we can find ways to grow closer to God through prayer. It means that we can know that prayer is much more than talking to God, but is our awareness of God's presence in our lives and our response to it.

Review

Scripture

Rejoice always. Pray without ceasing. In all circumstances give thanks, for this is the will of God for you in Christ Jesus.   (1 Thessalonians 5:16–18)

Prayer

Holy Spirit, you teach your people to pray through the guidance of the Church. Thank you for showing me so many ways to be in prayerful communion with you and with the Father and with Jesus. Help me to find the way to pray that is best for me right now in my life. Help me to grow in my prayer life so that I may better recognize God's presence in my life and respond by loving him and by loving my neighbors. Amen.

Chapter Highlights

- There are many different ways to pray.
- Vocal prayer includes traditional prayers and spontaneous prayer.
- Meditation, or reflective prayer, includes the Daily Examen, the Rosary, the Stations of the Cross, and *lectio divina*.
- Centering prayer is a type of contemplative prayer.

Terms to Remember

meditation   **Stations of the Cross**

React

Why do you think it is helpful to use the many different kinds of prayer you learned about?

_____

_____

At Home

Discuss this question with a grown-up. Write your answer.

How do you think the world would be different if all people prayed for peace every day?

_____

_____

_____

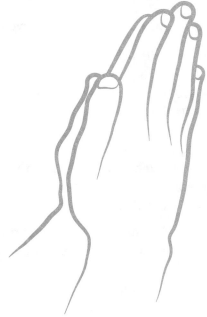

CHAPTER 18

The Lord's Prayer and How Prayer Works

 What does the phrase "to know by heart" mean?

It means that you have something memorized so well that you can say it without even thinking, like your phone number, address, or the multiplication tables. Catholics know many prayers by heart. What prayers do you know by heart? It is good to know prayers by heart, but we still have to remember to think carefully about those words. When we have a delicious dinner on the table, we might rush through praying grace so that we can start eating. If we take a moment to slow down and think about the words as we pray, it gives much more meaning to these prayers.

What Prayer Is and What It Isn't

Here's a quick review of what we know about prayer.

- Prayer is not us looking for God's attention. It is our responding to God's invitation.
- We do not pray to change God's mind. We pray to change ourselves.
- We don't use prayer to control or change what is reality.
- Prayer affects the person praying more than the person being prayed for.
- The effects of prayer cannot always be seen immediately.
- Prayer is not about getting what you want but accepting what God wants.

> We do not pray to change God's mind. We pray to change ourselves.

We pray because we love God and want to be close to him. We can also pray for those who do not believe in God. We pray that those people can hear that God is calling them and inviting them to know God.

At a Loss for Words

Most of the time, prayer can seem so simple. Other times it can seem very complicated. Saint Ignatius of Loyola, the founder of the Society of Jesus (the Jesuits), encouraged his followers to pray to God like you would talk to any of your friends. Prayer should be simple, but sometimes we don't know what words to use. We don't know how to listen or what we are listening for. The Holy Spirit, through the Church, gives us some help when it comes to prayer. Although prayer is simple, we might not know what to say or how to say it to God.

Think and Write

Have you ever tried to pray and couldn't find the words? What did you do?

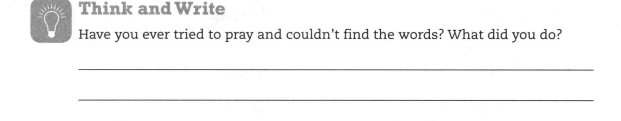

_____

_____

_____

Lord, Teach Us to Pray

Even Jesus' disciples knew what it was like to be at a loss for words when it came to prayer. So they went to Jesus and asked him if he could teach them how to pray. Jesus responded by teaching them the Our Father, which is also called the Lord's Prayer (Matthew 6:9–13). In this short prayer of only 55 words, Jesus gives us the words to use to talk to God.

Our Father, who art in heaven,
hallowed be thy name;
thy Kingdom come;
thy will be done
on earth as it is in heaven.
Give us this day our daily bread;
and forgive us our trespasses
as we forgive those who trespass against us;
and lead us not into temptation,
but deliver us from evil.

Think and Write

Think about what the words of this prayer mean. Write what you think you are saying as you pray each line of the Lord's Prayer.

Facts of Our Faith: *We Can't Change God's Mind*

In Genesis 18:16–33 and Exodus 32:1–14, we find stories that seem as if Abraham and Moses changed God's mind through prayer. In these stories, Abraham and Moses seem to convince God not to punish people because of their sins. However, in these stories, God is trying to teach them (and us) to follow God's will, which is always mercy. God taught Abraham and Moses to ask for God's help for those who needed it. They were seeking the mercy that God has always shown. These stories teach that God is a God of action and that he is involved in our lives. He draws people closer to him in their time of need.

_____

_____

_____

_____

_____

_____

_____

_____

What We're Really Saying

Let's take a closer look at just what we are saying in the Lord's Prayer.

- **Our Father** Not "my" but "our" Father. The first word of this prayer teaches us that if we have the same father, we must be brothers and sisters. To call God "Father" is to show that we know him and are close to him. We are not calling on a God that we do not know, but one who is our Father and knows us as his children.

- **who art in heaven** These words are not about *where* God is, but are about God's presence to us—for Heaven is nothing other than being fully in the presence of God. These words are words of praise.

- **hallowed be thy name** This is the first of seven **petitions,** or requests, which make up the rest of the Lord's Prayer. *Hallowed* is another word for *holy.* Our petition is that God's name will be honored and kept holy by all people. These words state that God's name is holy and that they serve as a petition that we keep God's name holy. As God's children and as people who are called Christians, we are praying that God's holiness will be shown to the world through our faithfulness to Jesus.

- **thy kingdom come** We declare our dependence on the king—God. This means that we will live as members of God's kingdom and follow his rule. God's kingdom is in our hearts and minds. We pray that God, who is love, will reign over all people and that we will depend on him.

- **thy will be done on earth as it is in heaven** Prayer is not about what we want, but it is about aligning ourselves with or doing God's will. Jesus is the supreme example of what it means to live according to God's will. In Heaven—in the presence of God—God's will is done faithfully. We pray that we might follow God's will.

- **Give us this day our daily bread** We pray that all people will have the basic necessities of life like food and shelter.

- **and forgive us our trespasses as we forgive those who trespass against us** We ask for God's forgiveness, but only if we forgive others in the same way that we have already been forgiven by Jesus. In this petition, we recognize that God's mercy cannot be felt in our hearts if we are still unforgiving toward others.

- **and lead us not into temptation** We ask God to help us stay out of trouble.

- **but deliver us from evil** We need to be saved from evil and sin, and only God's grace and love can do that.

In this very special prayer, we praise God and ask for what we need. There are seven petitions. The first three are about God. These help us draw close to him: thy name, thy kingdom, thy will. They say that we honor him and will follow him. The last four petitions are about us and what we need from God: give us, forgive us, lead us not, and deliver us. Praying this prayer helps us to become as humble and trusting as Jesus.

Facts of Our Faith: *Is God Male?*

People might think that God is male because we use the words *God our Father,* but God is neither male nor female. We call upon God as Father in the Lord's Prayer because that is the name revealed to us by Jesus. We can also describe God by using motherly characteristics because it gives us another idea of how loving and warm God is.

Live It!

When we pray the words "Give us this day our daily bread," we are asking God to provide food and spiritual nourishment for us and for all people. Write about one way you can live out this request to help others have what they need.

_____

_____

_____

_____

_____

So What?

So what difference does it make that Catholics pray the Lord's Prayer? It means that we can pray to the One who we know and who knows us— God our Father. It means that we pray in the words that Jesus himself gave us. It means that we pray with confidence, knowing that our prayers are heard. We know that as we pray these words, we are more closely aligning ourselves with God in whose image we are made.

Review

Scripture

"Ask and it will be given to you; seek and you will find; knock and the door will be opened to you. For everyone who asks, receives; and the one who seeks, finds; and to the one who knocks, the door will be opened."   (Matthew 7:7–8)

Prayer

Lord, Jesus, thank you for teaching me to pray. Holy Spirit, guide me and help me to pray without ceasing. Our Father who art in heaven, . . .

Chapter Highlights

- Jesus taught his disciples how to pray by teaching them the Lord's Prayer.
- Prayer is not about what we want, but what God wants for us.
- We do not pray to change God's mind, but to change ourselves.

Term to Remember

petition

React

Think about the seven petitions in the Lord's Prayer. Choose two and tell what they mean to you and how you can teach others what God wants for all people through these petitions.

_____

_____

At Home

Discuss this question with a grown-up. Write your answer.

If you had to tell about the Catholic faith in a short paragraph, what would you say Catholics believe?

_____

_____

Conclusion

While it's true that bridges take care of us, helping us safely cross over from one side to another, it's also true that we need to take care of bridges so that they don't weaken and collapse. When that happens, people can find themselves stuck on one side, unable to cross over to get to school or work or to buy food.

Throughout our lives, we also need to take care of the bridges of faith that take care of us. We need to keep them strong, making sure that no cracks form that will weaken them and allow them to collapse, leaving us stranded in a place where sin can harm us. How do we keep our bridges to faith strong? By constantly learning more about our faith, by celebrating the sacraments, by living a good moral life, and by praying.

Life is a long journey and we need long, strong bridges of faith to carry us to our destination, which is eternal life with Jesus. Your journey has only just begun. May you continue to walk with Jesus and invite others to join you along the way.

Prayers

Nicene Creed

I believe in one God,
the Father almighty,
maker of heaven and earth,
of all things visible and invisible.

I believe in one Lord Jesus Christ,
the Only Begotten Son of God,
born of the Father before all ages.
God from God, Light from Light,
true God from true God,
begotten, not made, consubstantial with the Father;
through him all things were made.
For us men and for our salvation
he came down from heaven,
and by the Holy Spirit was incarnate of the Virgin Mary,
and became man.

For our sake he was crucified under Pontius Pilate,
he suffered death and was buried,
and rose again on the third day
in accordance with the Scriptures.
He ascended into heaven
and is seated at the right hand of the Father.
He will come again in glory
to judge the living and the dead
and his kingdom will have no end.

I believe in the Holy Spirit, the Lord, the giver of life,
who proceeds from the Father and the Son,
who with the Father and the Son is adored and glorified,
who has spoken through the prophets.

I believe in one, holy, catholic and apostolic Church.
I confess one baptism for the forgiveness of sins
and I look forward to the resurrection of the dead
and the life of the world to come. Amen.

Apostles' Creed

I believe in God,
the Father almighty,
Creator of heaven and earth,
and in Jesus Christ, his only Son, our Lord,
who was conceived by the Holy Spirit,
born of the Virgin Mary,
suffered under Pontius Pilate,
was crucified, died and was buried;
he descended into hell;
on the third day he rose again from the dead;
he ascended into heaven,
and is seated at the right hand of God the
    Father almighty;
from there he will come to judge the living and
    the dead.

I believe in the Holy Spirit,
the holy catholic Church,
the communion of saints,
the forgiveness of sins,
the resurrection of the body,
and life everlasting. Amen.

Hail Mary

Hail Mary, full of grace,
the Lord is with you.
Blessed are you among women,
and blessed is the fruit of your womb, Jesus.
Holy Mary, Mother of God,
pray for us sinners,
now and at the hour of our death. Amen.

Lord's Prayer

Our Father, who art in heaven,
hallowed be thy name;
thy kingdom come,
thy will be done
on earth as it is in heaven.
Give us this day our daily bread,
and forgive us our trespasses
as we forgive those who trespass against us;
and lead us not into temptation,
but deliver us from evil.
Amen.

Act of Contrition

My God,
I am sorry for my sins with all my heart.
In choosing to do wrong
and failing to do good,
I have sinned against you
whom I should love above all things.
I firmly intend, with your help,
to do penance,
to sin no more,
and to avoid whatever leads me to sin.
Our Savior Jesus Christ
suffered and died for us.
In his name, my God, have mercy.

Hail, Holy Queen *(Salve Regina)*

Hail, holy Queen, Mother of mercy,
hail, our life, our sweetness, and our hope.
To you we cry, the children of Eve;
to you we send up our sighs,
mourning and weeping in this land of exile.
Turn, then, most gracious advocate,
your eyes of mercy toward us;
lead us home at last
and show us the blessed fruit of your womb, Jesus:
O clement, O loving, O sweet Virgin Mary.

Confiteor (Penitential Act)

I confess to almighty God
and to you, my brothers and sisters,
that I have greatly sinned
in my thoughts and in my words,
in what I have done and in what I have failed to do,

    (and, striking their breast, they say:)

through my fault, through my fault,
through my most grievous fault;
therefore I ask blessed Mary ever-Virgin,
all the Angels and Saints,
and you, my brothers and sisters,
to pray for me to the Lord our God.

Glory Be to the Father

Glory be to the Father,
and to the Son,
and to the Holy Spirit.
As it was in the beginning,
is now, and ever shall be,
world without end.
Amen.

Sign of the Cross √

In the name of the Father,
and of the Son,
and of the Holy Spirit.
Amen.

Glossary

Advent the four weeks before Christmas. It is a time of joyful preparation for the celebration of the Incarnation, Jesus' birth as our Savior.

apostolic one of the four Marks of the Church. The Church is apostolic because it hands on the teachings of the apostles through their successors, the bishops.

Baptism one of the three Sacraments of Initiation. Baptism frees us from Original Sin and gives us new life in Jesus Christ through the Holy Spirit.

bishop a man who has received the fullness of Holy Orders. As a successor to the original apostles, he takes care of the Church and is a principal teacher in it.

Beatitudes the ways we can behave to live a blessed life. Jesus teaches us that if we live according to the Beatitudes, we will live a happy Christian life.

catholic one of the four Marks of the Church. The Church is catholic because Jesus is fully present in it and because Jesus has given the Church to the whole world.

Christian the name given to all those who have been anointed through the gift of the Holy Spirit in Baptism and have become followers of Jesus Christ

Christmas the feast of the birth of Jesus (December 25)

commandment a standard, or rule, for living as God wants us to live. Jesus summarized all the commandments into two: love God and love your neighbor.

Communion of Saints the union of all who have been saved in Jesus Christ, both those who are alive and those who have died

community Christians who are gathered in the name of Jesus Christ to receive his grace and live according to his values

Confirmation the sacrament that completes the grace we receive in Baptism. Confirmation seals, or confirms, this grace through the seven Gifts of the Holy Spirit that we receive as part of Confirmation. This sacrament also unites us more closely in Jesus Christ.

conscience the inner voice that helps each of us to know the law that God has placed in our hearts. It guides us to do good and avoid evil.

Corporal Works of Mercy kind acts by which we help our neighbors with their everyday material needs. Corporal Works of Mercy include feeding the hungry, giving drink to the thirsty, clothing the naked, sheltering the homeless, visiting the sick and the imprisoned, and burying the dead.

covenant a solemn agreement between people or between people and God. God made covenants with humanity through agreements with Noah, Abraham, and Moses. These covenants offered Salvation. God's new and final covenant was established through Jesus' life, Death, Resurrection, and Ascension.

deacon a man ordained through the Sacrament of Holy Orders to the ministry of service in the Church. Deacons help the bishop and priests by serving in the various charitable ministries of the Church.

disciple a person who has accepted Jesus' message and tries to live as Jesus did

Easter the celebration of the bodily raising of Jesus Christ from the dead. Easter is the festival of our redemption and the central Christian feast.

ecumenism the movement for unity among Christians. Christ gave the Church the gift of unity from the beginning, but over the centuries that unity has been broken. All Christians are called by their common Baptism to pray and to work to maintain, reinforce, and perfect the unity Christ wants for the Church.

Epiphany the day on which we celebrate the visit of the Magi to Jesus after his birth. This is the day that Jesus was revealed as the Savior of the whole world.

Eucharist the sacrament in which we give thanks to God for giving us the Body and Blood of Jesus Christ. This sacrament brings us into union with Jesus Christ and his saving Death and Resurrection.

evangelization the proclamation, or declaring by word and by example, of the good news about the Salvation we have received in Jesus Christ. Evangelization is a sharing of our faith with others, both those who do not know Jesus and those who are called to follow Jesus more closely.

examination of conscience the act of prayerfully thinking about what we have said or done that may have hurt our relationship with God or with others. An examination of conscience is an important part of preparing to celebrate the Sacrament of Penance and Reconciliation.

excommunication a severe penalty that is imposed by the Church authorities for serious crimes against the Catholic religion. A person who is excommunicated is excluded from participating in the Eucharist and the other sacraments and from ministry in the Church.

free will our ability to choose to do good because God has made us like him

grace the gift from God given to us without our deserving it. Sanctifying grace fills us with God's life and enables us always to be his friends. Grace also helps us to live as God wants us to live.

Holy Week the celebration of the events surrounding Jesus' suffering, Death, Resurrection, and establishment of the Eucharist. Holy Week commemorates Jesus' triumphal entry into Jerusalem on Palm Sunday, the gift of himself in the Eucharist on Holy Thursday, his Death on Good Friday, and his Resurrection at the Easter Vigil on Holy Saturday.

humility not taking undue pride in our own achievements as all our gifts and talents come from God.

justice the strong, firm desire to give to God and others what is due them. Justice is one of the four central human virtues, called the Cardinal Virtues, by which we guide our Christian life.

laity those who have been made members of Christ in Baptism and who participate in the priestly, prophetic, and kingly functions of Christ in his mission to the whole world. The laity is distinct from the clergy, whose members are set apart as ministers to serve the Church.

Lent six weeks during which we prepare to celebrate, with special prayers and action, the rising of Jesus from the dead at Easter. Jesus rose from the dead to save us.

liturgical calendar the calendar that tells us when to celebrate the feasts of Jesus' birth, life, Death, Resurrection, and Ascension

liturgy the public prayer of the Church that celebrates the wonderful things God has done for us in Jesus Christ

Magisterium the living, teaching office of the Church. This office, through the bishops and with the pope, provides an authentic interpretation of the Word of God. It ensures faithfulness to the teaching of the apostles in matters of faith and morals.

Marks of the Church the four most important characteristics of the Church. The Church is one, holy, catholic, and apostolic.

Mary Magdalene a follower of Jesus who accompanied Christ and ministered to him (Luke 8:2–30). She was present at the foot of the cross, witnessed Christ being placed in the tomb, and is the first witness to his Resurrection (Matthew 28:1–10; Mark 16:1–8; Luke 24:10). She is especially noted for her encounter with the risen Jesus in the Gospel of John (John 20:1–18).

Matrimony a solemn agreement between a woman and a man to be partners for life, both for their own good and for raising children. Marriage is a sacrament when the agreement is properly made between baptized Christians.

meditation a form of prayer using silence and listening that seeks through imagination, emotion, and desire to understand and respond to what God is asking.

Memorare a prayer of petition for Mary, the Mother of God's intercession on behalf of her children. In the prayer the petitioner seeks Mary's protection, inspired by complete confidence in Mary's willingness to help.

mercy the gift to be able to respond to those in need with care and compassion. The gift of mercy is a grace given to us by Jesus Christ.

Missal the liturgical book that contains the texts and the rites for the celebration of the Mass in the Roman Rite of the Catholic Church.

moral choice a choice to do what is right or not do what is wrong. We make moral choices because they are what we believe God wants and because we have the freedom to choose what is right and avoid what is wrong.

Nicene Creed the summary of Christian beliefs developed by the bishops at the first two councils of the Church, held in A.D. 325 and 381. It is the Creed shared by most Christians in the East and in the West.

Noah According to Genesis 6:9, Noah was a righteous man who walked with God. As such, in the midst of a corrupt world, Noah was chosen to lead his family into the ark with a variety of animals. The ark was a place of refuge built by Noah on God's command to protect him and his family from the universal flood that God sent upon the earth.

Ordinary Time the part of the liturgical year outside of the seasons and feasts and the preparation for them

Paschal Mystery the work of Salvation accomplished by Jesus Christ through his Passion, Death, Resurrection, and Ascension. The Paschal Mystery is celebrated in the liturgy of the Church. We experience its saving effects in the sacraments.

penance the turning away from sin with a desire to change our life and more closely live the way God wants us to live. We express our penance externally by praying, fasting, and helping those who are poor. This is also the name of the action that the priest asks us to take or the prayers that he asks us to pray after he absolves us in the Sacrament of Penance and Reconciliation.

Pentecost the 50th day after Jesus was raised from the dead. On this day, the Holy Spirit was sent from Heaven, and the Church was born.

petition a request of God, asking him to fulfill a need. When we share in God's saving love, we understand that every need is one that we can ask God to help us with through petition.

prayer the raising of our hearts and minds to God. We are able to speak to and listen to God in prayer because he teaches us how to do so.

priest a man who has accepted God's special call to serve the Church by guiding it and building it up through the ministry of the Word and the celebration of the sacraments

prodigal son The second son in Jesus' parable in Luke 15:11–32, who demands his inheritance from his father. He leaves and spends the money wastefully and, deserted by his so-called friends, ends up in abject poverty. He repents, returns to his father, and experiences the power of unconditional forgiveness.

Promised Land the land first promised by God to Abraham. It was to this land that God told Moses to lead the Chosen People after they were freed from slavery in Egypt and received the Ten Commandments at Mount Sinai.

Purgatory a state of final cleansing after death of all our human imperfections to prepare us to enter into the joy of God's presence in Heaven

Redeemer Jesus Christ, whose life, Death on the cross, Resurrection from the dead, and Ascension into Heaven set us free from sin and brings us redemption

redemption our being set free from sin through the life, Death on the cross, Resurrection from the dead, and Ascension into Heaven of Jesus Christ

Resurrection the bodily raising of Jesus Christ from the dead on the third day after his Death on the cross. The Resurrection is the crowning truth of our faith.

Revelation God's communication of himself to us through the words and deeds he has used throughout history. Revelation shows us the mystery of his plan for our Salvation in his Son, Jesus Christ.

rite one of the many forms followed in celebrating liturgy in the Church. A rite may differ according to the culture or country where it is celebrated. *Rite* also means "the special form for celebrating each sacrament."

sacrament one of seven ways through which God's life enters our lives through the work of the Holy Spirit. Jesus gave us three sacraments that bring us into the Church: Baptism, Confirmation, and the Eucharist. He gave us two sacraments that bring us healing: Penance and Reconciliation and the Anointing of the Sick. He also gave us two sacraments that help members serve the community: Matrimony and Holy Orders.

sacramental object, prayer, or blessing given by the Church to help us grow in our spiritual life

sacrifice a ritual offering of animals or produce made to God by the priest in the Temple in Jerusalem. Sacrifice was a sign of the people's adoration of God, giving thanks to God, or asking for his forgiveness. Sacrifice also showed union with God. The great high priest, Christ, accomplished our redemption through the perfect sacrifice of his Death on the cross.

saint holy person who has died united with God. The Church has said that these people are now with God forever in Heaven.

Salvation the gift of forgiveness of sin and the restoration of friendship with God. God alone can give us Salvation.

sanctifying grace the gift of God, given to us without our earning it, that unites us with the life of the Trinity and heals our human nature, wounded by sin. Sanctifying grace continues the work of making us holy that began at our Baptism.

Scripture the holy writings of Jews and Christians collected in the Old and New Testaments of the Bible

sin a choice we make that offends God and hurts our relationships with others. Some sin is mortal and needs to be confessed in the Sacrament of Penance and Reconciliation. Other sin is venial, or less serious.

social justice the fair and equal treatment of every member of society. Social justice is required by the dignity and freedom of every person, and it is rooted in the Bible as well as in the traditional teachings of the Church.

solidarity the principle that all people exist in equal dignity as children of God. Therefore, individuals are called to commit themselves to working for the common good in sharing material and spiritual goods.

Spiritual Works of Mercy the kind acts through which we help our neighbors meet needs that are more than material. The Spiritual Works of Mercy include counseling the doubtful, instructing the ignorant, admonishing sinners, comforting the afflicted, forgiving offenses, bearing wrongs patiently, and praying for the living and the dead.

Stations of the Cross a tool for meditating on the final hours of Jesus' life, from his condemnation by Pilate to his Death and burial. We do this by moving to representations of 14 incidents, each one based on the traditional sites in Jerusalem where these incidents took place.

stewardship the careful and responsible management of something entrusted to one's care, especially the goods of creation, which are intended for the whole human race. The sixth Precept of the Church makes clear our part in this stewardship by requiring us to provide for the material needs of the Church, according to our abilities.

Tradition the beliefs and practices of the Church that are passed down from one generation to the next under the guidance of the Holy Spirit. What Christ entrusted to the apostles was handed on to others both orally and in writing.

Triduum the period of three days that begins with the Mass of the Lord's Supper on Holy Thursday evening and ends with the Easter Vigil Mass on Holy Saturday.

Trinity the mystery of one God existing in three Persons: the Father, the Son, and the Holy Spirit

viaticum the Eucharist that a seriously ill or dying person receives. It is spiritual food for the last journey we make as Christians, the journey through death to eternal life.

virtue attitude or way of acting that help us do good

vocation the call each of us has in life to be the person God wants us to be. Our vocation is also the way we serve the Church and the Kingdom of God. Each of us can live out his or her vocation as a layperson, as a member of a religious community, or as a member of the clergy.

worship the adoration and honor given to God in public prayer

Name _____ Date_____

1. The four pillars of the Catholic faith are
   a. sacraments, Eucharist, the Lord's Father, and prayer.
   b. Baptism, Marriage, Confirmation, and Holy Orders.
   c. the Creed, sacraments, the moral life, and prayer.

2. In the Creed, we
   a. say what we believe.
   b. pray for forgiveness.
   c. pray to show thanks.

3. The sacraments are
   a. sacred signs of our faith.
   b. separate from God.
   c. gestures and objects used in prayer.

4. To live a moral life, we should
   a. bend the rules.
   b. follow the Ten Commandments.
   c. do what our friends do.

5. Prayer is
   a. both speaking and listening to God.
   b. only speaking to God.
   c. only done during Mass.

6. Our Catholic faith is about
   a. making friends.
   b. listening to our priest.
   c. having a relationship with God.

7. Abraham and Sarah, Moses, and Mary
   a. didn't know God.
   b. said yes to God's call.
   c. turned away from God.

8. Revelation is
   a. Jesus dying and rising on Easter Sunday.
   b. God showing himself to us so that we can be close to him.
   c. honoring Mary.

9. Humility is
   a. recognizing that all our gifts and talents come from God.
   b. telling everyone what a good job we did.
   c. a quality that only saints have.

10. The Church believes in God's Revelation in
    a. Scripture, but not Tradition.
    b. Tradition, but not Scripture.
    c. both Scripture and Tradition.

Name _____ Date_____

11. The Immaculate Conception is Mary's
    a. being taken up to Heaven.
    b. being conceived free from Original Sin.
    c. being told by the angel Gabriel that she was to be the mother of the Son of God.

12. The Trinity is
    a. any group of three friends.
    b. not something we must believe in.
    c. God the Father, Son, and Holy Spirit.

13. We are made in the image of
    a. our parents.
    b. God.
    c. Mary and the saints.

14. Through his Resurrection, Jesus
    a. became Catholic.
    b. overcame death and sin.
    c. was tempted to sin.

15. Salvation is
    a. a gift.
    b. something you develop as an adult.
    c. not possible on earth.

16. Faith in Jesus
    a. is important only when we are worried or scared.
    b. must be earned.
    c. gives us hope for the future and for a new life.

17. Stewardship is
    a. sharing our time, talent, and treasure.
    b. sharing our toys, books, and money.
    c. sharing our food, clothes, and time.

18. We can become more spiritual by
    a. keeping track of our good works.
    b. writing down prayers.
    c. learning to find God in all things.

19. The Marks of the Church are that it is
    a. one, holy, catholic, and apostolic.
    b. trinity, holy, universal, and apostolic.
    c. Father, Son, and Holy Spirit.

20. The Communion of Saints is made up of
    a. only people whom the Church has named as saints.
    b. anyone who has died.
    c. saints and people who faithfully followed Jesus in their lives.

Name _____ Date_____

1. Liturgy is
   a. worshiping with others in our parish.
   b. an act of service.
   c. donating money to the church.

2. The Sacraments of Initiation are
   a. Penance, Matrimony, and the Eucharist.
   b. Baptism, Confirmation, and the Eucharist.
   c. Holy Orders and the Anointing of the Sick.

3. The Paschal Mystery is
   a. the Resurrection.
   b. the Crucifixion.
   c. the suffering, Death, and Resurrection of Christ.

4. The Sacraments of Healing are
   a. Penance and Reconciliation and the Anointing of the Sick.
   b. Holy Orders and Matrimony.
   c. Baptism and Matrimony.

5. Sacramentals are
   a. objects like holy cards and rosaries that help us draw our attention to God.
   b. things we worship.
   c. not useful for prayer.

6. The liturgical calendar
   a. is a sacrament schedule.
   b. is a list of days we honor Mary.
   c. highlights the seasons and feasts in the Church year.

7. In the Eucharist,
   a. we are sealed with the Holy Spirit.
   b. we receive the Body and Blood of Jesus Christ.
   c. we entered into a new life in the Church.

8. At Confirmation we
   a. become members of the Church.
   b. are sealed with the Holy Spirit.
   c. receive Holy Communion for the first time.

9. Baptism
   a. frees us from Original Sin.
   b. can be received more than once.
   c. is only for adults.

10. Two Gifts of the Holy Spirit are
    a. peace and understanding.
    b. love and hope.
    c. wisdom and knowledge.

Name _____ Date_____

11. An examination of conscience is
   a. how the priest forgives our sins.
   b. the act of looking prayerfully into our hearts to ask how we have hurt our relationship with God or with others.
   c. a sacramental celebration.

12. Charity, gentleness, and self-control are
   a. Fruits of the Holy Spirit.
   b. Gifts of the Holy Spirit.
   c. qualities of all Catholics.

13. The Sacrament of Penance and Reconciliation
   a. is something we receive only once.
   b. is not necessary.
   c. restores our relationship with God.

14. The Sacrament of Penance and Reconciliation includes
   a. confession, adoration, reconciliation, and prayer.
   b. contrition, confession, absolution, and satisfaction.
   c. contrition, healing, Communion, and penance.

15. The Sacrament of the Anointing of the Sick can be given
   a. to people preparing for surgery and people who are seriously ill.
   b. when someone has a cold.
   c. only to those who are very old.

16. The bishop is the head of
   a. a school.
   b. a diocese.
   c. a nation.

17. In the Sacrament of Matrimony,
   a. the couple forms a covenant with each other and with God.
   b. the priest marries the couple.
   c. sins are forgiven.

18. The Church encourages us to receive the Eucharist
   a. once a week.
   b. as often as possible.
   c. once a year.

19. Which liturgical symbol is used at Confirmation?
   a. water
   b. candle
   c. sacred Chrism

20. Men who help continue Jesus' presence on earth in the tradition of the apostles receive the Sacrament of
   a. the Eucharist.
   b. Holy Orders.
   c. Matrimony.

Name _____ Date_____

1. Christian morality is
   a. doing whatever we want to do.
   b. treating others with respect and dignity.
   c. not worrying about other people's feelings.

2. "Whatever you did for one of these least brothers of mine, you did for me" (Matthew 25:40) means
   a. when we serve others, we serve Jesus.
   b. take care of the people in your family.
   c. don't worry about those who are poor.

3. Catholic morality helps us
   a. focus on our needs.
   b. learn about the Bible.
   c. grow closer to God.

4. Grace is
   a. something we have to earn.
   b. a gift from God.
   c. a gift from the saints.

5. When we sin, we
   a. choose to do something we know God wouldn't want us to do.
   b. accidentally do something wrong.
   c. only hurt ourselves.

6. The Ten Commandments
   a. tell us how to maintain a relationship with God and others.
   b. are laws that we follow when we want to.
   c. are rules that Jesus gave us.

7. What is the Great Commandment?
   a. Love God and love your neighbor as yourself.
   b. Love your family and then love your friends.
   c. Love yourself.

8. The first three commandments teach us about
   a. the Church.
   b. the love of neighbor.
   c. the love of God.

9. The last seven commandments teach us about
   a. the love of God.
   b. the love of neighbor.
   c. the Gospels.

10. Jesus gave us ways for how God wants us to live by loving our neighbors. These ways are called
    a. the Beatitudes.
    b. prayers.
    c. rules for living.

Name _____ Date_____

11. Which virtue gives us confidence that God will always be with us?

    a. justice

    b. fortitude

    c. hope

12. Mercy is

    a. believing that we are better than others.

    b. showing compassion and forgiveness.

    c. not sharing with others.

13. The Spiritual Works of Mercy

    a. provide for the spiritual and emotional needs of people.

    b. help those who are hungry and homeless.

    c. are practiced only by priests.

14. What is the Eighth Commandment?

    a. You shall not bear false witness against your neighbor.

    b. You shall not covet your neighbor's goods.

    c. You shall not take the name of the Lord your God in vain.

15. What is the Fourth Commandment?

    a. You shall not steal.

    b. Honor your father and your mother.

    c. Keep holy the Sabbath day.

16. Life and Dignity of the Human Person and Care for God's Creation are two

    a. Catholic Social Teaching principles.

    b. Beatitudes.

    c. Cardinal Virtues.

17. Which are some ways that help form a good conscience?

    a. Do what your friends want you to do.

    b. Pray to the Holy Spirit, learn from your mistakes, and read and listen to Scripture.

    c. Wait until you are an adult to form your conscience.

18. Charity is also called

    a. faith.

    b. love.

    c. temperance.

19. The virtues of faith, hope, and charity are called the

    a. Cardinal Virtues.

    b. Theological Virtues.

    c. Beatitudes.

20. Your conscience is

    a. not helpful for making good choices.

    b. something you develop as an adult.

    c. what guides you to do the right thing.

Name _____ Date_____

1. Prayer is
   a. a response to God.
   b. trying to get God's attention.
   c. something we do only when we are in trouble.

2. Adoration, petition, intercession, thanksgiving, and praise are known as
   a. forms of prayer.
   b. things you do during the Sacrament of Penance and Reconciliation.
   c. examination of prayer.

3. In prayers of intercession, we are
   a. praying for the needs of others.
   b. asking God to take care of our own needs.
   c. praising God.

4. Prayer describes
   a. what happens to us at Mass.
   b. all the ways we recognize God's presence.
   c. only the Rosary.

5. During the Rosary, we reflect on the Joyful, Luminous, Sorrowful, and Glorious
   a. Stations.
   b. Prayers.
   c. Mysteries.

6. The following are traditional prayers:
   a. the Apostles' Creed, the Hail Mary, and the Lord's Prayer.
   b. spontaneous prayer and meditation.
   c. contemplation and reflection.

7. Spontaneous prayer is
   a. reading a Scripture passage.
   b. repeating a sacred word or phrase.
   c. praying using our own words.

8. The steps of spontaneous prayer are
   a. give thanks, identify your needs, forgive and be forgiven, and think of others.
   b. go to Church, identify your name, forgive others, think before you act.
   c. give thanks, identify your needs, forgive, and talk to God.

9. Meditation is
   a. using Scripture passages, inspirational readings, or sacred images to think about God.
   b. saying traditional prayers aloud.
   c. using our own words to pray.

10. The Catholic practice of devotion to Mary that reflects on the life of Jesus and Mary is called
    a. the Rosary.
    b. the Stations of the Cross.
    c. *lectio divina.*

Name _____ Date_____

11. We use our senses and imagination to reflect on Jesus' Passion, Death, and Resurrection in
   a. the Daily Examen.
   b. the Hail Mary.
   c. the Stations of the Cross.

12. The Daily Examen was developed by
   a. Jesus.
   b. Saint Paul.
   c. Saint Ignatius of Loyola.

13. Reflective prayer is also known as
   a. contemplation.
   b. vocal prayer.
   c. meditation.

14. In centering prayer, we
   a. open our hearts and minds to God's presence in silence.
   b. use traditional prayers.
   c. use rosary beads.

15. The Stations of the Cross
   a. has 12 stations.
   b. is also called *lectio divina*.
   c. sometimes includes a 15th station that reflects on Jesus' Resurrection.

16. The Lord's Prayer is also called the
   a. Our Father.
   b. Act of Contrition.
   c. Apostles' Creed.

17. Why do we pray?
   a. to get credit for doing something good
   b. because we love God and want to be close to him
   c. because the Church tells us to pray

18. When Jesus' disciples asked him if he could teach them to pray, he taught them
   a. to use their own words.
   b. the Our Father.
   c. the Apostles' Creed.

19. When we pray the Lord's Prayer, we ask God to forgive us
   a. as we forgive those who have sinned against us.
   b. as he forgave the disciples.
   c. as he forgives the sins of our fathers.

20. When we say "Give us this day our daily bread," we are asking
   a. God to forgive us.
   b. God to help us avoid evil.
   c. God to provide for the basic needs of all people.

Index

Scripture Index